Preparing to Adopt

A TRAINING PACK FOR PREPARATION GROUPS IN ENGLAND

Elaine Dibben, Eileen Fursland and Nicky Probert

Preparing to Adopt consists of:
- A Trainer's Guide with a CD-ROM
- A DVD of film clips
- An Applicant's Workbook

Training the Trainers

BAAF is able to assist you with delivering this training course. We can offer Training the Trainers courses in England.

If you would like more details, please contact Kanu Patel on 0121 753 2001 or email kanu.patel@baaf.org.uk.

BAAF
ADOPTION & FOSTERING

Published by
British Association for Adoption & Fostering (BAAF)
Saffron House
6–10 Kirby Street
London EC1N 8TS

www.baaf.org.uk

Charity registration 275689 (England and Wales) and SC039337 (Scotland)

© BAAF, 2002, 2006, 2010, 2014
Second edition, 2006
Third edition, 2010
Fourth edition, 2014

British Library Cataloguing in Publication Data
A catalogue record for this book is available from
the British Library

ISBN 978 1 910039 12 0

Project management by Shaila Shah, Director of Publications, BAAF
Designed by Helen Joubert Design
Printed in Great Britain by The Lavenham Press

Photos © iStockphoto, posed by models, except for photographs on pages 60, 61 and 62.

All rights reserved. Apart from any fair dealing for the purposes of research or private study, or criticism or review, as permitted under the Copyright, Designs and Patents Act 1988, this publication may not be reproduced, stored in a retrieval system, or transmitted in any form or by any means, without the prior written permission of the publishers.

The moral right of the authors has been asserted in accordance with the Copyright, Designs and Patents Act 1988.

BAAF is the leading UK-wide membership organisation for all those concerned with adoption, fostering and child care issues.

Contents

INTRODUCTION	**1**
The need for adoption preparation	1
The present position	1
Changes to adoption training and assessment	2
The adoption preparation and assessment process	3
Stage One	3
Stage Two	3
Matching and family-finding	4
This edition of Preparing to Adopt	5
What this pack comprises	7
The relationship between preparation and assessment	8
How much prior knowledge is assumed?	8
The scope of this course	9
Additional modules	10
Who should train and group size	11
Setting the "tone"	12
To get the best from this preparation course	13
Tips for trainers	13
Some strategies for trainers	15
Ground rules	17
What you will need for each session	18
The key qualities and capacities that prospective adopters need	18
Introductory/warm-up exercises	19
AN ADDITIONAL RESOURCE FOR YOUR INFORMATION EVENING	**23**
Quiz: Who can adopt?	23
MODULE 1	**27**
What is adoption?	**27**
Learning outcomes	27
EXERCISE: The meaning of adoption	28
PRESENTATION: What is adoption?	29
Routes to adoption	30
EXERCISE: What we have to offer	33
PRESENTATION: What do we need in order to become adoptive parents?	34
EXERCISE: What a child loses	35
HANDOUT: Lexy's story	36
PRESENTATION: Providing a secure base for an adopted child	38
PRESENTATION: The child's journey to adoption	39

MODULE 2   43

The children   43

    Learning outcomes   43
    EXERCISE: Meet some children   44
    PRESENTATION/DISCUSSION: Why do children need adoptive families?   51
    PRESENTATION: Characteristics of children needing adoption   52
    HANDOUT: Who are the children?   53
    PRESENTATION: The children needing adoption   55
    PRESENTATION: 'When can we see the children?'   60

MODULE 3   65

The adoption process   65

    Learning outcomes   65
    PRESENTATION: The agency   66
    PRESENTATION: Your journey to adoption   66
    EXERCISE: What is adoption like for a child?   67
    PRESENTATION: The assessment process   68
    PRESENTATION: How a child is identified and matched with you   70
    PRESENTATION: Learning about you and your family   71
    EXERCISE: Why adoption support is vital   72
    PRESENTATION: Adoption support   73
    PRESENTATION: Support from this agency   75

MODULE 4   77

Children's development and attachment   77

    Learning outcomes   77
    PRESENTATION: Children's development   78
    HANDOUT: Quiz: Children's development   78
    HANDOUT: Children's development: answers to quiz   79
    PRESENTATION: Reciprocity   79
    PRESENTATION: Attachment   80
    PRESENTATION: A child's damaged attachments: implications for adopters   88
    EXERCISE: The effect of repeated separations on a child   91
    PRESENTATION: Loss and grief   93
    EXERCISE: The bricks in the wall   95
    EXERCISE: Who am I?   97
    EXERCISE: Children and identity distortion   98

MODULE 5 — 102

The needs of children affected by neglect and abuse — 102

Learning outcomes — 103
PRESENTATION: Neglect and abuse — 103
EXERCISE: Tina's story — 103
HANDOUT: Tina's story — 104
PRESENTATION: What do "neglect" and "abuse" actually look like? — 105
EXERCISE: Who's looking at you? — 110
PRESENTATION: How trauma affects attachments and brain development — 110
PRESENTATION AND GROUP EXERCISE: Helping children through your day-to-day care — 116
PRESENTATION: Attending: providing the child with positive attention — 126
EXERCISE: Attending — 127
PRESENTATION: Building resilience — 128
EXERCISE: Promoting resilience — 129
PRESENTATION: Therapeutic intervention as part of post-adoption support — 130

MODULE 6 — 136

Becoming a parent through adoption — 136

Learning outcomes — 136
EXERCISE: How and why have you come to the point in your life when you are considering adoption? — 137
PRESENTATION: Our expectations and the reality — 137
EXERCISE: Considering children — 140
PRESENTATION FROM INVITED SPEAKER(S): Children with disabilities — 140
EXERCISE: What do you need to be a parent? — 142
PRESENTATION: What do you need to be an adoptive parent? — 142
Sibling groups — 144

MODULE 7 — 147

Linking, matching and introductions — 147

Learning outcomes — 147
PRESENTATION: Linking and matching — 148
PRESENTATION: Introductions for children of different ages — 158
EXERCISE: Cultural differences — 162
PRESENTATION: Matching...and children's identity needs — 162
PRESENTATION: Life story work — 164

MODULE 8 — 169

Telling, contact and social networking — 169

    Learning outcomes — 169
    PRESENTATION: Talking about adoption with your child — 170
    EXERCISE: When to tell and what to tell — 171
    HANDOUT: Jordan — 171
    PRESENTATION: Thinking about birth families — 172
    PRESENTATION: Contact — 174
    PRESENTATION: Helping children with contact — 181
    HANDOUT: Jasmine — 183
    PRESENTATION AND QUICK-THINKS: The internet and e-safety for children — 184
    PRESENTATION: Your child's story — 185
    PRESENTATION: Social networking issues in adoption — 186

MODULE 9 — 193

Life as an adoptive family: learning to live together — 193

    Learning outcomes — 193
    EXERCISE: What you are looking forward to — 194
    PRESENTATION: What if you don't feel love for the child? — 195
    EXERCISE: The origins of challenging behaviour in children — 196
    HANDOUTS — 197
    PRESENTATION: Positive interventions — 199
    PRESENTATIONS FROM INVITED SPEAKERS: Support for adoptive families — 201
    PRESENTATION: Adopted children in school — 202

CD-ROM Contents

Powerpoint presentation
Handouts
    Reading list for applicants
    Course evaluation form

DVD Contents

Module 1	Two families talk about their adoption experiences	3.50 mins
	A family with a birth daughter talk about adopting a little boy	2.0 mins
	A couple talk about life with their adopted son	0.50 mins
	Chantelle reads a poem: ADOPTION	0.34 mins
Module 2	Three Stories: One family – three children talk about their adoption	7.30 mins
	An introduction to Adoption Activity Days	2.30 mins
	Scenes from an Adoption Activity Day	1.40 mins
	Information about Be My Parent	1.20 mins
	Information about the Adoption Register and Exchange Days	5.0 mins
Module 3	Jade and Jordan talk about becoming adopted and what adoption means for them	9.36 mins
	Children and young people talk about their wait to be adopted and life with their adoptive family	11.35 mins
Module 4	Serve and return interaction shapes brain circuitry – Illustrates reciprocity between parent and child	1.41 mins
	The arousal/relaxation cycle – introduced by Gillian Schofield	5.07 mins
	Heather and Ayesha talk about their lives in their adoptive families	1.40 mins
Module 5	Toxic stress derails healthy development	1.50 mins
	The science of neglect	5.50 mins
	Executive functioning: Skills for life and learning	5.20 mins
	Experts discuss the effects of neglect and abuse on children and how parents can help – John Simmonds and Kate Cairns in conversation	9.50 mins
	Parents' experiences of adoption	3.08 mins
	A father's experience of adoption	1.05 mins
Module 6	Prospective adopters undertake exercises to explore motivation to adopt, their relationships and the kinds of children who would be suitable	5.0 mins
Module 8	A birth mother talks about having her child adopted	6.0 mins
	An adopted young person talks about contact with her siblings and its significance	8.20 mins
	Adopted adults discuss their curiosity about their birth family and whether or not they want to trace them	8.05 mins
Module 9	How adoption changed their lives: Three families share their experiences	1.30 mins

Acknowledgements

This edition of *Preparing to Adopt* draws on earlier editions of the course, and we would like to thank everyone who has contributed to those editions in any way over the last 12 years. It also owes a debt to the research and writing of many adoption practitioners, researchers, authors and others too numerous to mention here but whose work you will see quoted and acknowledged throughout the text.

The first edition of *Preparing to Adopt*, published in 2002, was devised by a working party from BAAF including Pat Beesley, Barbara Hutchinson, Ian Millar and Sushila de Sousa and it was written up by Eileen Fursland. A number of colleagues from BAAF assisted with preparing revised editions: Sushila de Sousa and Ian Millar contributed to the second edition published in 2006; Marjorie Morrison, Katrina Wilson, Karen Wilkins and Shaila Shah (BAAF's Director of Publications) contributed to the third edition in 2009.

For this new and largely rewritten edition of *Preparing to Adopt*, our grateful thanks go to Chris Christophides and Laura Williams (BAAF Trainer/Consultants) and Katrina Wilson for their input; Berni Stringer (BAAF Central England) for materials relating to attachment; adoption practitioners Marian Eagleson from Coventry and Hazel Field from Adoption Matters North West, for their feedback on the draft copy; Jo Francis for her assistance; and of course Shaila Shah for her input into the content, for the editing, and for bringing this new edition to publication. Shaila also compiled the *Applicant's Workbook* that accompanies this *Trainer's Guide*.

Notes about the authors

Elaine Dibben

Elaine Dibben started her social work career in residential social work and qualified in 1988. She has over 20 years' experience of working in adoption and fostering in local authority and voluntary adoption agency settings and is a strong advocate for the importance of securing permanence in family settings for children who cannot return to their parents' care.

She joined BAAF in 2004 to become manager of the Independent Review Mechanism, which she set up and ran until 2009, when she moved to take on a wider role in BAAF as a trainer/consultant. She is currently an Adoption Development Consultant for BAAF alongside acting as a panel Chair for both adoption and fostering panels.

She has written several good practice guides that have been published by BAAF – *Devising a Placement Plan* (2012), *Parent and Child Fostering*, with Paul Adams (2011), *Undertaking an Adoption Assessment in England* (second edition 2013), and *Completing a Child Permanence Report in England* (2014).

She lives in Oxfordshire with her husband, Steve.

Eileen Fursland

Eileen Fursland is a freelance writer specialising in issues affecting children and young people. She has written extensively for BAAF on a number of publications, as well as for a range of magazines and national newspapers and other organisations. Eileen wrote the training pack for the first edition of *Preparing to Adopt* in 2002, working with the original working party from BAAF which devised the course.

Eileen's publications for BAAF include her books *Facing up to Facebook* (second edition 2013); *Social Networking and Contact* (2010); *Foster Care and Social Networking* (2011); a booklet for young people, *Social Networking and You* (second edition, 2013); and *Ten Top Tips on Supporting Education*, with Kate Cairns and Chris Stanway. In earlier collaborations with Kate Cairns, she co-wrote BAAF's training programmes, *Trauma and Recovery; Safer Caring; Building Identity;* and *Transitions and Endings*.

Eileen also provides training sessions on the implications of social networking for adoption and fostering and how to manage the challenges it poses. She delivers workshops for social workers and adopters at the request of local authorities and other adoption organisations (www.create-and-communicate.com). Since the publication of the books on social networking, she has had speaking and training engagements on this issue in England, Wales, Scotland, Northern Ireland, the Republic of Ireland, Italy and Belgium.

Nicky Probert

Nicky Probert gained a Master's degree in Social Work and qualified as a social worker in 1985 after spending the early part of her career in London, working with children and young people in residential care and the youth justice system. She then worked in several London boroughs within family placement services. On moving to the Midlands, Nicky worked directly with children and young people, doing life story work and post-abuse counselling and conducting risk assessments with families.

Nicky has been working in family placements for over 25 years and helped to set up a new adoption service where she became team manager, as well as devising preparation courses for adopters and child protection distance learning courses for foster carers. She joined BAAF in 2003 to help disseminate and share best practice with colleagues involved in social care.

Whilst remaining a strong advocate for permanency for children, she also recognises the importance of early intervention to give birth families the support they need to parent effectively and to protect children from harm. She believes passionately in professionals ensuring that they hear the voice of the child.

Nicky has two adult children from her first marriage and currently lives in Birmingham with her partner and his daughter.

INTRODUCTION

The need for adoption preparation

For anyone considering adoption, in-depth preparation is vital. It provides the opportunity to find out what adoption involves and to develop the skills that will be required as an adoptive parent. It also helps the person to reflect on what adoption would mean for them.

High-quality preparation, skilfully delivered, helps prospective adopters to:

- consider what adoption actually entails, for them and for a child;
- decide whether adoption is right for them and their family, and think about the kind of child/children they might adopt;
- gain a greater understanding of the needs of the children awaiting adoption;
- learn how they, as adoptive parents, could meet a child's needs;
- appreciate the nature of adoption as a lifelong process;
- identify any areas in which they need to develop in order to be approved as adopters.

The present position

In 2011, the Westminster Government embarked on a major programme of adoption reform following concerns about the delays being experienced by children where adoption had been identified as the right plan for them to achieve permanence and the increasing number of those children who were then not achieving adoption.

The other related concern was the need to encourage more prospective adopters to come forward for the children waiting for adoption and to ensure that they then experienced a timely response in terms of information, preparation and training to equip them for their parenting role and a quality assessment of their ability to parent children who have experienced trauma and abuse prior to their adoption placement.

In England, there is now monitoring of local authority performance in achieving timely placements for children being placed for adoption and these results are published annually through the adoption scorecard system. From 2014, it is anticipated that there will be similar reporting on the progress of the adopter's journey. The introduction of a new two-stage assessment process that incorporates elements of preparation and training in both stages, means that agencies will need to be able to offer more flexible and collaborative arrangements to enable preparation to be delivered during these shortened timescales. The two-stage process applies to both domestic and intercountry prospective adopters.

From April 2013, there has been an equalisation of the inter-authority and inter-agency fee paid between adoption agencies for the work undertaken to prepare, assess and support prospective adopters and a legislative requirement introduced so that children and families waiting more than three months must now be referred to the Adoption Register to provide maximum opportunity for a successful match. An increased emphasis on the importance of recruiting for the national rather than local need and continuing development of regional

Preparing to adopt

consortia of adoption agencies will mean that agencies must have confidence in the content and delivery of the preparation and training of adopters carried out by colleagues in other agencies.

Changes to adoption training and assessment

In 2012–13, the Government made a number of changes to both adoption preparation and assessment. The aim was to improve the adoption process. The changes came about because of concerns that some people were being deterred from adoption because of what they perceived to be a lengthy and intrusive approval process or because they believed they would not be eligible to adopt.

- The First4Adoption telephone helpline and website were set up as a first port of call for anyone interested in finding out more about adoption. First4Adoption is supported and funded by the Department for Education. Advisers from First4Adoption provide general information, help prospective adopters to find adoption agencies and talk them through the options.

- The processes of application, preparation and assessment have been divided into two parts and new timescales have been introduced: two months for Stage One and four for Stage Two (see below).

- Applicants may, if they wish, decide to take a break of up to six months between the end of Stage One and beginning Stage Two.

- The Prospective Adopter's Report (England) (BAAF, 2013) has been revised and streamlined in order to reduce the duplication of information, with a stronger emphasis on the summarising and analysis of information by the social worker undertaking the assessment.

Other Government initiatives to speed up the adoption process and encourage more people to adopt include:

- the "adoption map" of England, which shows the average waiting times for children to be adopted, by local authority area;

- adoption "scorecards", which rank local authorities in terms of the time taken to place children with adoptive families, and rank agencies for their assessment of adopters;

- the Government's "adoption passport", which sets out the support available for those who want to adopt a child. Adopters could be eligible for paid adoption leave, priority access to social housing, priority admission for school places and support services such as counselling;

- the proposed introduction of "personal budgets" for adopters to purchase whatever kind of adoption support they feel would most benefit them and their child, from a range of providers including voluntary adoption agencies and adoption support agencies.

Introduction

The adoption preparation and assessment process

- People interested in adoption can find out more about it from individual local authorities and adoption agencies or by using the First4Adoption telephone helpline or website. They may also wish to read introductory guides on adoption or narratives describing people's adoption experiences. (We have provided a reading list for applicants, which is available in the Applicant's Workbook, and BAAF, First4Adoption and Adoption UK websites also suggest lists of suitable titles.) People considering adoption may contact a number of agencies in order to find the agency with which they are most comfortable; they then make a single formal application to that agency.

- Many agencies will offer prospective applicants an informal meeting with a social worker or the opportunity to attend an information evening before they decide to register their interest in starting the assessment process. The informal meeting or information evening will help them understand what the agency has to offer and flag up any potential obstacles to their eligibility early on in the process.

Stage One

This stage is "adopter-led" and should normally take no longer than two months. It involves the applicant finding out more about adoption by doing their own research and by attending preparation groups, while the agency completes some required checks.

- When a prospective adopter has made a formal Registration of Interest (ROI), the applicant and agency agree a Prospective Adopter Stage One Plan, setting out both parties' responsibilities and expectations for this stage of the process. The agency asks the applicant for some basic factual information about them and their household, income, occupation, health and so on; contact details of referees; and some basic information on the kind of child they might consider adopting.

- The agency will take up references, carry out a check for a criminal record (DBS), and ask applicants to have a medical examination completed by their GP.

- Applicants are invited to attend preparation groups with other prospective adopters.

- Based on the information gathered during this period (Stage One) the agency makes a decision on whether the applicant can continue to the assessment and training stage (Stage Two).

- If the agency decides an applicant is unsuitable to adopt, they must provide a clear explanation of the reasons why they will not be able to progress to Stage Two.

Stage Two

This stage is "agency-led" and involves the formal assessment and more in-depth preparation.

Preparing to adopt

- Stage Two should be completed within four months.

- Once the applicant has told the agency that he/she wishes to proceed to assessment, the applicant and the agency agree a prospective adopter assessment plan detailing the assessment process and dates of meetings and training sessions. The agency will also set out its duties in relation to the assessment (the home study) and Prospective Adopter's Report (PAR).

- During this four-month period, applicants are assessed as well as having further training, and at the end of the four months the agency decides whether or not to approve.

- The PAR is required by legislation. As well as information gathered by the assessing social worker, it includes information provided by the applicant and the results of statutory and other checks that have been carried out.

- At the end of the assessment process, the assessing social worker gathers all the information together into the PAR, which is taken to the agency's independent adoption panel for a recommendation on the applicant's suitability to adopt.

- The applicant is provided with a copy of the PAR and has five working days in which to comment on it, if they wish, before it goes to panel.

- The panel recommendation is then considered by the agency decision-maker, who will decide to approve prospective adopters or issue a qualifying determination that they consider the applicant(s) are unsuitable to adopt.

Matching and family-finding

- Prospective and approved adopters are now encouraged to take on a more active role in seeking a match with suitable children who are awaiting adoption, for example, by looking at profiles of children and by attending adoption exchange events and activity days.

- Agencies must also prepare a Matching Plan in consultation with domestic adopters, including information about the duties of the agency in relation to placement and reviews and the role of the prospective adopter in identifying a child for whom they may be an appropriate match.

- Once adopters have been approved, agencies can refer them to the Adoption Register for England (which they are likely to do if they think there is a low chance of finding a suitable child in their region). Agencies *must* refer adopters to the Adoption Register three months after their approval if there is no prospect of a match in their region.

Introduction

This edition of *Preparing to Adopt*

Adoption preparation has changed, so this edition of *Preparing to Adopt* represents a significant change from previous editions. The course has been re-designed so that it is modular, providing more flexibility and allowing applicants to join the course at different stages. The modules have been designed to align with the two-stage adoption process.

The content of the preparation course has been updated with reference to the latest policy and guidance from the Department for Education as well as changes in practice such as "fostering for adoption" (FfA) and concurrent planning schemes. It has also been updated to reflect the complicated histories of the population of children who are currently waiting for adoptive families.

The course includes exercises involving children's profiles and case studies. Considering such profiles and case studies helps applicants to understand the characteristics and needs of children waiting for adoption, and it helps them to work out what matters to them most and what kind of child(ren) they would like to adopt.

Agencies are now making more use of initiatives such as Adoption Exchange events and Adoption Activity Days to bring together prospective adopters with children who are waiting. This change too is reflected in this updated edition.

This edition of *Preparing to Adopt* incorporates a great deal of new training material. There are new ideas for exercises, new case studies and a different format, which reflects the two-stage process. There is a greater emphasis on the effects of trauma, grief and loss on children who need adoption, but at the same time the rewards of adoptive parenthood are brought to the fore.

Trainers are directed to video clips available on the enclosed DVD and elsewhere to illustrate some of the points in the training. For example, they can show interviews with adopters (from BAAF's YouTube channel) which bring the joys of adoptive parenting to life; they can show clips of adopted children speaking about their experiences; and they are directed to educational videos made by other authoritative sources such as The Harvard Center on the Developing Child (in the US) to illustrate some important points.

Upcoming changes (at the time of writing) in the way that adoption support is provided are also incorporated into the new edition.

Society has seen other changes since the last edition of *Preparing to Adopt*, for example, the revolution in social networking, which has important implications for adoptive families. That too is covered here.

The format of *Preparing to Adopt*

The *Preparing to Adopt* course is made up of nine separate training modules which have been broadly designed to fit within the two-stage assessment process: we envisage that agencies will use the first three of these in their Stage One training and the following six in Stage Two. However, there is no requirement about what should be covered during Stages

Preparing to adopt

One and Two of the assessment process so agencies may want to structure the modules differently to fit with their proposed model of delivering preparation and training.

Each module has been designed to be self-contained; we see all the modules as an essential part of the training course apart from *Linking, matching and introductions*, which agencies may instead choose to deliver as a post-approval module.

The modules are listed below.

1. What is adoption?
2. The children
3. The adoption process
4. Children's development and attachment
5. The needs of children affected by neglect and abuse
6. Becoming a parent through adoption
7. Linking, matching and introductions
8. Telling, contact and social networking
9. Life as an adoptive family: learning to live together

Agencies may want to decide if there are certain modules that they require applicants to complete before they can continue to Stage Two.

As the course is modular, participants do not have to complete the sessions within each stage in a particular sequence. This allows participants to join and complete the preparation course at different times.

At the beginning of each module we give a guide to the duration of the module, but please note that this is an approximate timing. Timing is flexible and will vary depending on the size of the group, the extent to which the trainer goes into depth about the material, and the amount of questioning and discussion that arises during the session.

Depending on the time agencies decide to devote to training, this preparation course could run as separate sessions or two of the shorter sessions could be combined into a day's training. Since time for reflection is so important, it is not recommended that the modules are all run on consecutive days.

The course provides a range of opportunities to enhance participants' knowledge, understanding, interest and subsequent transfer of learning.

It includes numerous exercises in which participants participate actively and "learn by doing". Such exercises are likely to prove to be some of the most memorable parts of the preparation for participants. Time for group discussion is also vital. Participants value this and it allows them to learn and gain new insights by listening to other people's thoughts and experiences. Presentations – in which the trainer stands at the front and imparts information to the participants – should be kept brief.

Introduction

The wording on the PowerPoint slides has deliberately been kept as concise as possible. For a presentation to be effective, trainers must do more than simply read out what appears on slides. Where necessary, we have provided information for trainers to read in advance, so that they can expand on the summary provided on the slides.

What this pack comprises

- This trainers' guide, which contains instructions for running each training module, including:
  - the PowerPoint slides (also included on a CD-ROM affixed to the inside back cover);
  - information for trainers to help them expand on the content of the slides;
  - information for trainers on how to conduct the learning exercises;
  - recommendations for further reading around each topic;
  - material for handouts and exercises (also on the CD-ROM affixed to the inside back cover).
- A CD-ROM with the PowerPoint presentation, handouts and course evaluation form.
- A DVD with film clips.
- The Applicant's Workbook.

The PowerPoint slides and handouts are for display and distribution to those attending courses; they may not be used for other purposes and are copyrighted to BAAF unless otherwise indicated.

The Applicant's Workbook

Agencies should supply each applicant with an Applicant's Workbook prior to the course. The Workbook follows the modular structure of the preparation group programme. Each section contains useful articles, information, and worksheets to allow participants to continue to develop the themes of individual sessions. A reading list is also supplied.

The Workbook will build on the content of each module by providing further information and reading for the applicants and a dedicated space for them to record their thoughts and observations during the course.

Much of the course content is built around the idea of supporting prospective adopters to develop the knowledge and skills they will need in order to become adoptive parents. Some of the information in the Workbook will relate to parts of the Prospective Adopter's Report (PAR) – for example, it will explain how to complete the family support map and genogram, which applicants are expected to start in Stage One and complete in Stage Two with guidance from their social worker.

Completed worksheets from the Applicant's Workbook may prove to be a rich source of evidence to inform the assessment process.

Preparing to adopt

The relationship between preparation and assessment

There has been a lack of clarity in the past about the relationship between preparation of adopters and the assessment process. This has been made clearer with the publication of the Government's *An Action Plan for Adoption: Tackling delay* and the implementation of the two-stage process, which has been designed to offer 'initial training and preparation – clearly separated from the assessment process' (Department for Education, 2012). It is anticipated that prospective adopters will use initial preparation provided by their agency, along with online training materials being made available on the First4Adoption website and their own reading, research, learning and reflection, to develop their understanding of adoption and to consider what they have to offer before progressing to a full assessment in Stage Two.

Statutory adoption guidance indicates that all adopters should receive some preparation prior to their approval, which can be offered through groups or on an individual level and should take into account their existing experience and knowledge about adoption. The benefits of meeting and hearing from other adopters are also highlighted.

The content of this preparation is now set out in The Adoption Agencies (Miscellaneous Amendments) Regulations 2013 para 24 (2a–2f). It includes information about the range of children needing adoption; their likely needs and the background they may come from; the significance of adoption for a child and their family; information about post-adoption contact between a child and their birth family; the skills needed by adoptive parents and an understanding of the assessment process; and the child's journey through care through to their placement for adoption. This information is expected to equip prospective adopters to demonstrate their understanding of what adoption will mean to them and enable them to engage with their assessing social worker during their home study.

The information that is then required for the completion of the PAR includes an assessment of the prospective adopter's understanding of the issues involved in adoption and their parenting capacity to meet a child's emotional and behavioural needs and support a healthy development of the child's identity through understanding their previous history and appropriate contact with their birth family. This means that there is an assumption that adopters will have had input in these areas and an opportunity to reflect on them alongside and prior to the completion of their home study assessment.

While preparation can be offered separately from assessment, it will be important that prospective adopters are given the opportunity to reflect on and record their learning so as to share it with their assessing social worker and that there is open and transparent feedback from trainers involved in preparation so that any areas of vulnerability or further learning needs are discussed and highlighted in the assessment.

How much prior knowledge is assumed?

Applicants will join the course with widely varying levels of prior knowledge about adoption. Some will have read and researched in some depth, while others may have started exploring

Introduction

the subject only recently. In addition, because the course is modular, in any given session some participants may have attended one or two previous modules while others may be attending for the first time.

However, it can be assumed that everyone on the preparation course will, at the very least, have either:

- had a one-to-one conversation with a social worker about adoption;
- have attended an information session on adoption.

Even though everyone attending the course will have previously either spoken with a social worker or attended an information session, it's likely that not all of them will remember all the information they have been given. Discussing adoption evokes an emotional response and people may be concentrating on how they themselves come across to the social worker – both of which could interfere with their retention of information. So it is inevitable and perhaps necessary that trainers recap the basic information, especially in Stage One; they can go on to build on this.

Making the training interesting and relevant to a group with varying levels of knowledge is one of the challenges for the trainers delivering this course. Trainers should explicitly acknowledge that some participants may already be familiar with some of the information presented. Equally, trainers need to ensure that those who are new to the subject of adoption are not left feeling out of their depth because basic information has not been covered.

The scope of this course

This course is intended as initial training for anyone who wants to adopt in England and Wales (but the regulations and guidance are England-specific). It does not cover Scotland or Northern Ireland, although of course some of the training material will still be useful in those countries.

Naturally, a large part of the course is about the knowledge and skills needed to parent a child who has suffered trauma, grief and loss. However, it is impossible to cover everything an adopter would need to know in sufficient depth during the time available for this course. For example, if a first-time adopter is to be matched with a child who has experienced serious abuse and neglect, we envisage that post-approval training would be needed and provided and this will be covered in a collection of additional modules (see p 10) that will address specific issues in greater depth (to be published by BAAF in 2015). In addition, specialised courses are provided by a range of organisations including, for example, BAAF, Adoption UK and Family Futures.

People who wish to adopt a sibling group of two or more will find much in this course that will be helpful to them, but it is likely that they will need additional preparation and support. Trainers should ensure that they cater for the needs of prospective adopters of sibling groups as far as possible, for instance, by including practical information about the introduction process when adopting siblings, and strategies for coping with a sibling group.

Preparing to adopt

Trainers should ensure that they do not assume that everyone in the group will be adopting a single child – for instance, they should refer to "the child or children" rather than always "the child".

Some of the content of this course will be applicable to people in the above groups, but these applicants will also need further preparation specific to their situation including one-to-one preparation with a social worker, for example.

Intercountry adopters

The course is not intended for intercountry adopters, though some people intending to adopt a child from another country might benefit from it. There are a number of agencies that provide preparation courses specifically for prospective intercountry adopters.

Second-time adopters

One of the recent changes to the adoption system is that people who have already adopted a child do not need to go through the entire process again. Second-time adopters may go straight to Stage Two in some cases, or an agency might decide to run a special training course aimed at second-time (or third-time) adopters. Even if people have already adopted, they will still need the opportunity to reflect on how adopting another child or children will impact on their family and how the new child/children will find their place in the family.

Additional modules

BAAF will publish a collection of modules that could be offered to adopters needing to gain more knowledge about a particular aspect of adoption, during or post-approval. These will include the following.

- Adopting when you have birth children
- Foster carers wishing to adopt the child they are fostering
- Adopting a child with special needs
- Adopting a child of a different ethnicity and culture
- Adopting for a second time
- Adopting a child from abroad
- Adopting a sibling group
- Single adopters
- A module for adoptive grandparents, other family members and friends

Introduction

Who should train and group size

We expect that this course will be delivered by two trainers. It goes without saying that both of these trainers should have extensive knowledge about adoption. At least one trainer should be a family placement worker. The other might be, for example, an experienced adopter who ideally also has training skills or has been provided with some opportunity to develop these skills. Prospective adopters respond well to having this mix of experience and expertise in the trainers. We have included basic instructions on materials and resources needed for each session and on running the exercises.

The training sessions will probably work best with anything from eight to 20 participants.

Everyone is welcome

Participants come to the course with diverse backgrounds, ages, ethnicities, financial circumstances and sexual orientations. Whether applicants are single or married, bisexual, gay, heterosexual or transexual, and whatever their ethnicity or social class, trainers need to show that they are all welcome as prospective adopters.

Trainers need to be sensitive to the composition of the group, paying particular attention to how they will address the needs of applicants from minority ethnic groups, applicants with disabilities, single applicants, unmarried couples and gay and lesbian applicants. In some circumstances, it may be appropriate for agencies to consider joining forces to provide a training course geared to specific groups, for example, single applicants or people adopting a child from their extended family.

Trainers should ensure that they can cater for any special learning, dietary or religious needs by specifically asking applicants to let them know of these before attending the training sessions.

Here are some practical ways to ensure that your course is as inclusive as possible.

- The venue should be accessible to people with disabilities and wheelchair users.

- Language should not be a barrier so if English is not everyone's first language, be aware of the need to ensure that everyone has understood (do you need to provide an interpreter or a British Sign Language interpreter?).

- Check in advance whether any applicants have particular needs, for example, an applicant with impaired vision might need to sit close to the front and have the handouts printed in a larger type size or an applicant may need the use of a hearing loop.

- Don't refer automatically to "mums and dads" – especially if you have single applicants or gay couples in the group.

- Avoid scheduling training days on religious festivals and holidays, e.g. during Ramadan participants who are fasting may find a full day's training difficult.

- Ensure that a prayer room is available for applicants, where needed.

Preparing to adopt

- If providing refreshments, make sure these are acceptable to everyone, e.g. vegetarians and people who only eat gluten-free or kosher or halal food.
- Do not make assumptions about applicants' own histories – some may have suffered trauma themselves, been a child in care or adopted, or had a child adopted.

Issues of ethnicity and diversity, including issues for children with medical conditions and disabilities, will be included throughout the preparation course. Applicants who wish or plan to adopt a child of a different ethnicity or a child with a medical condition or disability will probably require further and more in-depth preparation than is given here. This could be provided pre- or post-approval either via an additional module or as individual preparation relating to a specific child they are being considered for.

Setting the "tone"

In the past, adoption preparation has been criticised by some who say that it focuses on the difficulties and presents scenarios of "doom and gloom". The Government is keen that adoption preparation should not deter prospective adopters and that it should include the positives about adoption.

Trainers will need to strike a careful balance here. As someone who is tasked with preparing prospective adopters, you owe it to them to ensure that they understand the demands and, yes, the risks of adoption. Of course, sometimes everything goes well, children are delightful and bring great rewards and joy to their adopters; but it must also be acknowledged that some children present huge challenges to their adopters and everyone else around them. Adoption changes lives, and that is true for adopters as well as for children. Adopters need to be prepared for this; indeed, this is one of the purposes of adoption preparation.

Inviting experienced adopters to address the group and using the DVD as well as some of the many online clips of positive interviews with adoptive families are good ways to accentuate the positives. Indeed, for the participants, hearing about the joys of adoptive parenting first-hand from an adopter may be more powerful and authentic than hearing it from a trainer. Be aware of the possibility that some participants might wonder whether you, as a representative of the agency, are giving them the "hard sell" because you are keen to increase the number of adopters. Explain that the aim of the preparation course (particularly in Stage One) is for people to find out more about adoption so that they can decide for themselves whether adoption would be right for them and their families.

Be aware of the balance of "light and shade". If the mood of the session appears to be getting too negative, be prepared to lift it with extra more positive anecdotes, exercises, clips, poems and so on. You will find some of these are provided, but it is a good idea for group leaders to have more ideas up their sleeves in case the mood of discussions/groups starts to become low and "stuck".

The decision to adopt a child is one of the most momentous that anyone can make. So we all owe it to applicants – and to the children they will go on to adopt – to ensure that they are as well prepared as possible for what lies ahead.

Introduction

To get the best from this preparation course

Agencies should ensure that course leaders:

- have been helped to develop the necessary training skills;
- have an understanding of adult learning principles;
- appreciate the principles underpinning co-training;
- are committed to anti-discriminatory practice;
- are familiar with the course content and are confident in delivering this.

Applicants should:

- be committed to attending the preparation groups and participating in them;
- be prepared to spend time before each session becoming familiar with the materials provided in the Applicant's Workbook;
- be prepared to give priority to any work to be undertaken between sessions;
- use their Workbook and the learning gained in the preparation groups to contribute to the home study/assessment.

Participants need to understand how the experience of this preparation course can tie in with and help them with the assessment process, so trainers should explain this (see page 8).

Tips for trainers

- If possible, choose a venue with good audio-visual facilities, i.e. a projector and a screen, and a whiteboard/flip chart.
- Send details of the venue, a map and information about public transport well in advance of the day.
- Provide a choice of drinks on arrival. Some people may have had long journeys to get to the training venue.
- First impressions count, so greet people in a friendly way when they arrive and introduce yourself. Chat informally to put them at their ease.
- Give out re-usable plastic name badges and collect them in each time. Get people to write their own names on their badges and that way you will know how they like to be referred to – for example, Charlie instead of Charles. Ask them to write their names in thick black pen so that you can read them from the front.
- Try to learn (or at least use) everyone's name if you can. If you learn and use only two or three people's names, some of the other participants may feel sidelined. If you find some people's names difficult, don't be afraid to ask them exactly how to pronounce their name.

Preparing to adopt

- Have an initial "welcome" slide projected on the screen, or write a "welcome" message on the flip chart. You could have some music playing in the background.

- Check that people are happy with the temperature of the room and, if necessary, adjust the heating or open the windows accordingly.

- Start on time – if you always wait for latecomers, people won't get the message that it is important to be punctual for the training sessions, and your timings will slip. (But you should still greet people in a friendly way when they arrive late – don't ruin the atmosphere for everyone by letting your frustration show!)

- At the start of each session, give an outline of what the training will involve – people like to know what kind of processes they will be engaged in during the event, and this may help to dispel any anxiety.

- Give participants handouts of the content (e.g. the PowerPoint slides and handouts) so that they don't feel they have to try to write everything down during the session.

- Always finish on (or ahead of) time. You can stay behind afterwards for informal chats with people who are not in a hurry to leave, but the session should finish at the advertised time so that people can leave to collect children, catch a bus or whatever, without feeling they are missing something.

- Remember that people need time to digest what they have heard. It often takes a while to take on board new ideas or concepts and feel comfortable with them, and this will certainly be true in adoption preparation.

- It might be a good idea to encourage participants to stay in touch with each other as they go through the process. You could get people who would like to do this to write their email addresses on a sheet, then give everyone a copy at the end.

- After each session, take some time to reflect on how you think it went and jot down some notes about what you learned, what went well and how you might do things differently next time. Once you've done this, make a conscious decision not to dwell on the negatives!

- Look carefully at the participants' responses on the evaluation forms and be prepared to adjust the training and the course activities in the light of this. Feedback is helpful, but again, try not to dwell on the pain of any negative feedback. Simply consider whether it is valid (e.g. negative feedback may have come from just one individual who was having a bad day!) and, if so, what you might do to improve things next time.

Participants' prior knowledge is one of your most important resources

As a trainer, you should welcome and capitalise on people's existing knowledge and experiences – make use of what they know. Involve the group and *allow group members to tell you things* whenever an opportunity presents itself and where this is appropriate. For example, a useful technique is to ask the group questions and invite group members to supply the answers, rather than presenting them with the information. That way, group members are active participants who are sharing their own knowledge with the group rather

Introduction

than passively sitting and (for some of them) being told things they already know. This method respects the knowledge and experience that some group members have already gained and prevents the more well-informed participants from feeling patronised. It also makes for a livelier and more interactive session. Whilst valuing those with knowledge and experience, it is also worth acknowledging that sometimes, those coming with "fresh eyes" can help us to reflect on why we do things as we do.

Working in groups

A good training event is mostly interactive – participants should not simply be sitting and listening for long periods.

Group discussion – in small groups or the whole group – actively involves the participants in coming up with varied ideas and approaches. It can help modify attitudes and clarify understanding as people learn from each other. Working in the safety of a small group helps some people to participate more than they might do otherwise.

Give couples the choice as to whether they work in the same small group or not.

It is sometimes useful to suggest gender-based groups (any transgender applicants can always self-select their group). In this way, men are often more able to reflect on emotional content, which is sometimes dominated by women in mixed groups.

Some strategies for trainers

- When giving presentations, remember how short people's attention spans are likely to be – keep the input brief and then invite questions.

- Small group discussions need to be carefully managed. Make sure everyone is clear about the task and the time allowed. Give them a "two-minute warning" when they need to bring their discussion to an end. If a particular group does not seem to be working well, i.e. either they are all too quiet or one or two members seem to dominate, split the groups in a different way for the next activity.

- You will need to support, guide and encourage people to express their views and consider those of others. When people are working in small groups, you shouldn't "sit in" on the group – this will change the dynamic. However, attending to what is going on in the group can sometimes be helpful to refocus the group on the task or to help those who are struggling. This needs a "light touch" approach.

- Value everyone's ideas and contributions. Remind them that in many cases there are no "right" answers. If the group is split on something, avoid taking sides – try to reflect everyone's views fairly. However, there will obviously be times when participants will ask for your views on important issues.

- To avoid direct confrontations from particularly challenging members of the group, it can be helpful to ask what the others in the group think, rather than get into a power struggle.

Preparing to adopt

- If anyone is having difficulty expressing what they want to say clearly, you may need to help them clarify it for the benefit of the rest of the group.

- Try to ensure that the group discussions involve the whole group and not just two or three people.

- Sometimes a group will contain an individual who always wants to talk about their own situation, or someone who has a lot of questions to ask and points to raise. Be careful not to let people like this hijack or dominate the group discussions – if necessary, offer to talk to them individually during the break or at the end of the session.

- Remember that a participant who seems "difficult" or argumentative may actually be feeling apprehensive and insecure. You could chat to them during the coffee break to try to find out what is bothering them.

- If someone has obvious misconceptions or is expressing views that are clearly wrong, you will need to query these if no one else does. Discriminatory remarks will also need to be challenged.

- Ask groups in advance to note their thoughts and suggestions on sheets of flip chart paper. Taking structured feedback helps you to check what people have learned and to correct any misconceptions, as well as sharing ideas with the rest of the group. You may wish to capture people's ideas on a flip chart (possibly with previously drawn sections, so that you can categorise ideas as you write them down). Where appropriate, refer back to the results of their feedback later in the session.

- Writing their feedback points on your flip chart shows that you value the group's work (even if the small group discussion itself is actually the main benefit).

- If small groups are all working on an identical task, avoid asking all the groups to feed back everything, as this can become repetitive. Instead, take one or two points from a group and then move on to the next group for one or two points from them. Or you could ask just one group to report back, then ask the other groups if there is anything they would like to add. Next time, choose a different group.

- If all the groups have missed something that really needs to be considered, you can address this in your summing-up at the end. Summarise people's views and ideas, make links, draw conclusions, and thank them for their contributions.

Taking questions

- It's a good idea to invite or welcome questions from the group during your talk – if you keep them waiting until the end, they may have lost interest.

- If someone asks you a question that you don't know the answer to, don't feel threatened. Thank them for raising an interesting issue. You could say you're not sure about the answer but promise to find out and get back to them. If appropriate, you could ask if anyone else in the room knows, or ask what the group thinks – you could write the question up on the flip chart and ask them to write any ideas they have on post-it notes and stick them on the flip chart sheet.

Introduction

Using visiting speakers

In some of the sessions it is suggested that someone other than the trainers is invited to come and talk to the group, such as an experienced adopter or a foster carer.

- If you invite someone in a telephone conversation, always follow this up in writing and confirm the date, time and venue and summarise the arrangements.

- Make sure the person understands exactly what you want them to cover, and in what way.

- Ensure that speakers are aware of confidentiality issues, i.e. when discussing any case examples in front of the group, these should be heavily anonymised.

- If they will be showing slides or giving out a handout, ask them to send these in advance so that you can make copies.

- Email a map of the location with directions about how to get to the venue, where to park, etc.

- During the person's talk, you may want to throw in a question or two of your own to help get things moving in the right direction or to help the group to understand something better.

- Always email or phone to thank the person after the event; you may also want to share some of the positive comments from the participants' evaluation forms.

Ground rules

You could invite participants to come up with their own "ground rules" for the way people behave and relate to each other during the training session, but during a short training event it is probably more sensible for you to save time by simply outlining some standard ground rules (you could write these up on a flip chart), then ask if anyone would like to add anything. There is a handout outlining these on the CD-ROM.

- Disagree with an idea or viewpoint – not with the person. Always treat others with respect.

- Everything that participants might hear from other participants within the training session should remain confidential and not be shared with anyone else.

- The only exception to this would be if a child protection issue comes to light, for example, if someone mentions something that seems to indicate that a child or young person whom they know is at risk. In this case, the information should be shared (with the trainer, who will take appropriate action).

- Trainers should say that they will keep information confidential unless it is to be shared with the assessing social worker as part of the assessment process. There will be feedback to inform the assessment, particularly in Stage Two. Trainers should make it clear how this works and what kind of information they might pass on. Make it clear that feedback will be shared openly and any concerns discussed with applicants.

Preparing to adopt

- Valuing diversity – if people on the course are a diverse group (in terms of ethnicity, age, background, single/married status and sexual orientation, for example) trainers should make it clear that they welcome everyone's differing perspectives and emphasise that everyone is valued for what they can bring to adoption.

- Anti-discriminatory practice – remind the group that no one should express discriminatory views or make unfavourable assumptions about other people's culture, ethnicity, religion, socio-economic status, family structure or sexual orientation. Make it clear that if any of the group members express any such views or use inappropriate language, they will be challenged.

What you will need for each session

- Name badges for trainers and participants
- Laptop computer, projector, speakers and screen
- The CD-ROM and DVD
- Any handouts printed off
- Flip charts and pens are always useful to write up key points
- Refreshments, if you are supplying these
- Any special aids you may need for people with disabilities, for example, a hearing induction loop

For certain sessions you may need to bring other resources for particular training exercises. These extra resources, if any, are listed at the start of each module.

You may wish to think about the most appropriate layout for your training room. Where possible, we would recommend a "cabaret" style with small groups of five or six around a table. This allows for small group exercises and discussions and helps people to feel more relaxed than either a more formal lecture theatre arrangement or a horseshoe shape, which can feel quite exposing. It also gives them space to put their Workbooks, take notes and write on flip chart sheets for various exercises.

The key qualities and capacities that prospective adopters need

Adopters need to be able to provide for the child's needs from placement through to adult life, including understanding the impact of maltreatment, loss or trauma on a child's development and responding to the needs that arise from these experiences.

The assessment of prospective adopters looks at their capacity to:

- build and sustain close relationships;
- empathise with and understand their own as well as other people's feelings, motives and behaviour;

Introduction

- resolve past traumas or losses, including infertility;
- build secure attachments;
- share difficulties and accept help.

The assessing social worker will also explore:

- whether a prospective adopter is likely to be able to help a child achieve their full educational potential, rather than expect the child to fulfil a particular set of expectations;
- whether a prospective adopter can support and encourage a child's identity and their growing sense of self as a separate and valued person, their view of their individuality, their abilities, self-image and self-esteem;
- the applicant's capacity to respond to likely scenarios, e.g. providing consistent emotional warmth to a child who rejects them and helping to improve a child's low self-esteem. The assessment should explore their willingness and capacity to look after a child who does not initially respond to boundaries and routines, who has learnt to survive in isolation and to reject emotional warmth, and whose behaviour might cause family conflict;
- the applicant's understanding of and agreement to the importance of telling the child that they were adopted and appropriately sharing what is known of their history and circumstances;
- the applicant's understanding of the significance of contact between an adopted child and their birth family members, as well as their views on what type of contact there should be, and with whom.

The assessment also looks at family and environmental factors that may impact on either the child's needs or the adoptive parenting capacities of the adopters.

Introductory/warm-up exercises

Some participants may be feeling slightly apprehensive or anxious, particularly at their first training session. In previous versions of this course, sessions were held sequentially and participants became an established group who got to know each other well as they progressed through the course. This course, in contrast, is modular. This means that there are likely to be different people attending each training module, and any of the Stage One sessions are likely to include some "first-timers", but this will depend on how your agency wants to deliver the course. So trainers should start each training session with a short introductory/warm-up exercise.

Some of the exercises below are designed to help people introduce themselves to the group and others are simply to put them at their ease. Trainers should aim to make these exercises informal, light-hearted and, if possible, fun!

Introductions should be kept short – the shorter the training session, the shorter the

Preparing to adopt

introductions should be. Here we provide a selection of eight warm-up exercises, each of which should take around five to 10 minutes (possibly longer with a large group). Trainers can select any introductory exercise of their choice to start each training module. Or they may, of course, have a favourite exercise of their own that they would like to use.

Trainers should consider providing some variety rather than using the same one or two warm-up exercises for all the modules.

Miming game

Participants stand in a circle. The trainer starts by saying his/her name and then 'I like...' and says something he/she likes to do (e.g. swimming), while simultaneously doing a mime of the activity. All the other members of the group should copy the mime at the same time.

The next person in the circle then says his/her name and adds an activity of their own while miming the appropriate actions, e.g. 'I like swimming and knitting'. The next person might add 'gardening' or 'cooking'. Both the individual person and the rest of the group should all do the mimes at the same time. The exercise continues, with the list of mimes to remember becoming longer all the time, until everyone in the group has had a turn. Hilarity should ensue!

'What did you have for breakfast?'

Participants pair up. They introduce themselves to each other and tell each other what they had for breakfast that day. Then each person in turn introduces their partner to the group as a whole, for example: 'This is Lindsay, she's a veterinary nurse and she had muesli followed by toast and honey...'

Introduce yourself in the time it takes...

For this exercise you need a box of matches (and a smoke alarm system that is not too sensitive!). One at a time, each person strikes a match and holds it up in front of them while introducing themselves to the group in the time it takes for the match to either burn out or get close to their fingers so that they have to blow it out.

This has two advantages: it keeps people's introductions short and it reduces people's self-consciousness – they are focusing on the match, rather than on the rest of the group, while they speak. (Alternatively, you could use some kind of timer such as an egg timer.)

Introduction

'What's the weather like?'

Participants stand in a circle but turn to the side so that each person is facing the back of the person in front of them. The trainer calls out the "weather" and people do the corresponding action on the back of the person who's in front of them. For instance, at the command: 'It's raining' everyone does a pitter-patter motion on the back of the person in front of them; "lightning" means drawing a zig-zag shape on the person's back; while "sunshine" means gently massaging their shoulders. You can come up with other suggestions for windy, hail, snow, etc.

The ball game

Participants need to be wearing their name badges for this game. They stand in a circle. The trainer starts by calling someone's name out while simultaneously throwing the ball to that person. The person catches the ball and then throws it to someone else in the circle, calling out their name at the same time. Continue until everyone has been included in the game at some point.

Guess the saying

Ask participants to divide into groups of three or four. Ask each group to come up with a well-known phrase or saying and then to make up a "clue" to what it is and write it down on a piece of paper (for example, 'Too many cooks spoil the broth' can become 'It's crowded in the kitchen'). Then each group should swap their "clue" with another group, and the groups try to work out the phrase or saying. Continue until each group has written down their guesses about all the phrases and then ask the groups to give their answers. Which group has guessed the most sayings and come out the winner?

Draw a picture

Ask participants to divide into small groups. Each person should draw a picture depicting something they hope for or are looking forward to. (Tell them that stick figures are fine!) For some, this may be a picture of them and the child or children they hope to adopt, any birth children they may have and perhaps their dog or cat. For others, it may be a picture of a holiday, wedding or big family party they are looking forward to, or a new home they hope to move to. Then ask them to share their picture with the other people in their small group and explain what their picture is about.

Play dough feelings

Give each participant a small amount of play dough and ask them to mould it into something to show how they are feeling. They then share this in pairs or small groups.

Preparing to adopt

Closing exercise

Trainers may wish to end each session with a short closing exercise. For example:

- Ask participants to spend a few minutes thinking about and making a note of three things that they have learned during the session and will take away with them.

- Ask participants to think about one thing that they have learned during the session that will help them, and one thing that they will need to think about or find out more about.

If time permits, you could ask participants to share their thoughts with others in a small group or ask for a couple of volunteers to share with the group as a whole.

Suggested reading for applicants

Direct participants to the reading list at the back of their Workbook. A copy of this is also available on the CD-ROM – print this off and hand out to participants.

Remind them of the importance of reading about adoption – both procedural guides and personal accounts – to get an idea as to what adoption means.

References and useful websites

BAAF (2013) *Prospective Adopter's Report (England): Guidance notes and additional resources*, London: BAAF

Department for Education (2012) *An Action Plan for Adoption: Tackling delay*, London: DfE

Adoption UK: www.adoptionuk.org.uk

BAAF: www.baaf.org.uk

First4Adoption: www.first4adoption.org.uk

AN ADDITIONAL RESOURCE FOR YOUR INFORMATION EVENING

At your information evening, you may wish to use the following quiz (presented as PowerPoint slides) to explain to participants the wide range of people who can now be considered as prospective adopters. (NB The figures are correct at the time of writing, but if you are using this quiz after 2014 you will need to provide up-to-date figures.)

Quiz: Who can adopt?

Show the following slides, each of which has a question about eligibility to be *considered* for adoption. After showing each slide, ask for a show of hands for the answer. Then provide participants with the answer.

SLIDE Will I be able to apply to adopt if I'm in my 40s?

Information for trainers

Yes! There is no upper age limit for people who want to be considered for adoption, and the average age for adopters is around 40. Many agencies prefer not to have an age gap of more than 45 years between the child and adoptive parent, but this can be flexible depending on the circumstances. (The lower age limit for being able to apply to adopt is 21.)

SLIDE My partner and I are living together but aren't married – will we be able to adopt?

Information for trainers

Yes. You do not have to be married or in a civil partnership in order to be considered as an adoptive parent. Recent statistics show that around 83 per cent of adoptions are by people either married or in civil partnerships. The rest will either be single or just living with their partner.

SLIDE Can I apply to be an adoptive parent if I am gay or lesbian?

Information for trainers

Yes. Being gay, lesbian, transgender or transsexual does not affect your right to be considered for adoption. Up to four per cent of children are adopted by same-sex couples, and some single adopters will also be gay or lesbian.

Preparing to adopt

SLIDE Can I become an adoptive parent if I already have birth children or step-children?

Information for trainers

Yes. However, agencies will normally want to have a gap of at least two years between the youngest child already in your family and an adopted child. This is to make sure that you will be able to attend to the individual needs of each child in the family.

SLIDE Do I have to be earning a certain amount or own my house before I can adopt?

Information for trainers

No. Your financial circumstances will be considered as part of the assessment process but low earnings, being on benefits or renting a house will not automatically rule you out from becoming an adoptive parent.

SLIDE Will having health problems or a disability affect my chances of becoming an adoptive parent?

Information for trainers

The key concern for agencies is to place a child or sibling group with adoptive parents who will be able to meet their needs through to adulthood and provide a stable family life. A medical examination will therefore be part of the assessment process for all applicants, and the impact of any current health condition or disability on your ability to care for a child will be given careful consideration.

SLIDE I am only interested in adopting a baby. How likely is it that this will be possible?

Informating for trainers

Nowadays there are very few babies being relinquished for adoption, although some are removed from their families as a result of concerns about neglect or abuse. The statistics show that only two per cent of children adopted in England were aged under one year (the figure is lower in Wales, and not available for Northern Ireland or Scotland), and that the

An additional resource for your information evening

average age at adoption is around three years and eight months. Therefore, restricting yourself to very young babies will mean it is less likely that you will be able to adopt.

SLIDE My partner and I are currently undergoing fertility treatment – does this mean we cannot also apply to adopt?

Information for trainers

Each case is considered on its merits. An agency may want you to wait for a period of time after you have finished fertility treatment. This is because undergoing unsuccessful fertility treatment can be difficult and emotional and you will need time to deal with these experiences before you can decide whether adoption is right for you and your family and commit yourself to the adoption process.

SLIDE I have a criminal record so should I assume that I won't be able to adopt?

Information for trainers

This is not the case. You will only be ruled out if you have a criminal conviction or caution for specified criminal offences against children, or some sexual offences against adults. However, you must disclose all convictions and cautions to your social worker so they can discuss with you any implications for children being placed and be prepared to look at this during your assessment, reflecting on the circumstances at the time and your learning from this since.

SLIDE What percentage of children are adopted by married heterosexual couples?

- 70 per cent?
- 80 per cent?
- 95 per cent?

Information for trainers

Over 80 per cent of adopters are married couples, but the number of adoptions by unmarried couples, civil partnership couples and single adopters is slowly increasing.

Preparing to adopt

SLIDE What percentage of people who are assessed end up being approved as adopters?

- 50 per cent?
- 60 per cent?
- 90 per cent?

Information for trainers

It is difficult to find figures for this but you can say that from a Department for Education survey of local authorities in 2013 (unpublished) we believe the closest figure is around 90 per cent. You will probably find that participants' suggestions are much lower. Point out that they should be encouraged by this!

Media reports about adoption sometimes feature people who have been turned down for some reason that the group may consider unjustified (e.g. being overweight). Explain to the group that such cases are rare and that, in any case, media reports may exaggerate or not tell the whole story. Explain why health does matter if a particular condition is likely to impact on a person's life expectancy and ability to look after a child long term.

Try to reassure the group as a whole by being positive about the chances of eventually being approved (obviously without pre-judging any individual's or individual couple's prospects).

SLIDE Is adoption for me?

Information for trainers

Some of the people in the group may be afraid of being rejected, for various reasons – try to reassure them and emphasise that everyone in the room has the right to be considered as a prospective adoptive parent.

The assessment process looks at whether they would be able to meet the needs of a child who is waiting for adoption.

Tell the group that they may still have some doubt in their minds about whether or not to continue with their application and that is only natural. Reassure them that, if they decide to continue, you fully expect them to be able to answer this question. Adoption is not for everyone. They are here to find out more and to decide whether adoption is right for them.

MODULE 1

What is adoption?

Timing

This module will take approximately three hours, not including any refreshment breaks. If you have a large group, there will be more questions and more discussion so it is likely to take longer.

Setting the scene

- Introduce yourself and explain your role in the agency. Explain to the group that the aim of this adoption preparation is to give them a realistic idea of the task ahead. It will also help them to decide whether adoption is something they want to do and are ready for.

- Remind the group of how your agency is structuring the course and where this module fits in – for instance, you may wish to explain that this is one of three training modules in Stage One of the adoption process and that the other modules are entitled *The Children* (which will tell participants more about the kind of children who need adoption) and *The Adoption Process*. However, your agency may be structuring the course differently.

- Refer to housekeeping issues (for example, fire escapes, toilets, timing of breaks and the time the session will end).

- Explain and outline the ground rules listed in the Introduction on page 17.

What you will need

For the exercise *What a child loses* in this module, you will need to provide a doll. You may also wish to have some copies of the leaflet *Fostering for Adoption: Becoming a carer* (Simmonds, 2013) to give out to participants at the appropriate point during the module. You can obtain copies from www.baaf.org.uk/ webfm_send/3216.

Introductions/warm-up exercise

Choose one of the exercises listed on pp 24–26 to put the group at their ease and to get them to introduce themselves to each other.

Learning outcomes

Show the slide below to explain the learning outcomes for this module.

Preparing to adopt

SLIDE Learning outcomes

This module will help you to:

- Understand what adoption means
- Understand the different paths to adoption
- Consider the qualities and capacities adopters need to have
- Consider the child's journey to adoption

Exercise

The meaning of adoption

Write up the word ADOPTION lengthways on a flip chart and, for each letter of the word, ask participants to suggest words beginning with that letter that come to mind when they think about adoption.

For example: anxiety, assessment; dad, delight; options, obstacles; PAR (Prospective Adopters' Report), parents, pleasure; training, testing; intense, interrogate; older; nature, nurture. If it seems that all the words being suggested have negative connotations, encourage participants to think of some positive words too!

After a couple of minutes, when you have a good selection of words, circle the negative words, then the positives.

Discuss the words, covering these key points.

- Adoption brings positives and negatives for everyone involved, for the rest of their lives.

- Adoption always involves loss as well as gain, for the child, the adopters and the birth parents. Encourage participants to consider the gains and losses for the child.

- Adoptive families will have many experiences in common with all other families – but some of their experiences and challenges will be different from those of other families.

- Encourage participants to think about the public perception of adoption. One of the differences for adoptive families is that their life becomes "public property". Adoption is the subject of comment in newspapers and on television programmes; it forms story lines in soap operas and is used as an instrument in achieving social policy aims.

Explain that this course will help them to think about what adoption means and to gain a deeper understanding of what it involves.

What is adoption?

Presentation

What is adoption?

SLIDE What is adoption?

Children whose birth family cannot provide them with a secure, stable and permanent home are entitled to have adoption considered for them.

SLIDE About adoption

- Adoption is for children who cannot stay with their birth families.
- Adoption is permanent.
- Adopters have the same parental rights and responsibilities as other parents.
- Adoptions today are rarely completely "closed".

Information for trainers

Both long-term fostering and adoption offer the child stability and security into adulthood, but in adoption the child is legally part of the adoptive family. Adoption is a legal procedure in which all parental rights and responsibilities for the child are permanently transferred by the court from the birth parents and/or the local authority to the adoptive parents. It is illegal to adopt a child without being assessed and approved by a UK adoption agency, although there are some circumstances (where a child is living with close relatives or existing foster carers) where a direct application can be made to the court.

Once an adoption order has been granted by the court (which makes the adoption legal), the adoptive parents have full legal responsibility for the child. This means they are the child's legal parents and make all decisions about the child's future. A new adoption certificate for the child is issued by the General Registrar's office and entered into the Adopted Children Register.

An **adoption order** cannot be *applied* for until a child has had a home with his or her adoptive parents, continuously, for at least ten weeks in England and Wales, and cannot be *made* by the court for 13 weeks in Northern Ireland and Scotland – although, in reality, most families have the order granted around nine to 12 months after the child moves in. Where children have already been living with their short-term foster carers or carers providing fostering for adoption (FfA) placements for more than 10 weeks, then their carers can make an adoption application once the placement for adoption has been formalised.

Preparing to adopt

In most cases in England and Wales, unless a child's birth parents formally consent to their child being adopted, the local authority caring for them must apply for a placement order from the court to allow the child to be placed for adoption.

In a "closed" adoption there is no contact between the birth family and the adoptive family, for the child's safety. However, in most adoptions there is some form of contact with birth relatives, which is usually arranged under a voluntary agreement with adopters. (Contact is discussed further in Module 8.)

There will be more information about contact in Stage Two preparation and training.

SLIDE Why might the birth family be unable to look after their child?

The birth parent(s) may have:

- Substance abuse issues
- Serious mental illness
- Learning difficulties
- History of violence and/or offences against children
- Domestic violence between adults in the home
- Other complex reasons why they are unable or unwilling to keep their child.

Information for trainers

It's unlikely that any participants will have come even this far without being aware that there are few babies available for adoption who are healthy, with no question marks over their development, who have been voluntarily given up by their birth parents. However, it is worth checking that everyone in the group understands that there are few babies who need adoption and that most of the children have been removed from their birth parents because of neglect or abuse or a high level of risk.

Routes to adoption

- Explain that there are three different routes to adoption, and elaborate on each of these.
- Explain that concurrent planning and fostering for adoption can be particularly emotionally challenging paths to adoption and they are not suitable for everyone.
- Tell the group that if anyone thinks they might be interested in these forms of adoption, they will be given the opportunity to explore them with a social worker later in the process.

What is adoption?

SLIDE Three paths to adoption

- Adoption from care
- Fostering for adoption
- Concurrent planning

Information for trainers

It may be helpful here to distribute leaflets explaining fostering for adoption and concurrent planning, if you have them.

1. Adoption from care: the most common path to adoption

- Child is removed from birth parents and taken into care
- Child lives with foster carers for duration of care proceedings
- Serious search for adopters does not begin until after the placement order
- When suitable adoptive parents are found, child is matched and placed with them
- When the adoption order is granted, the adoption is final

2. Fostering for adoption

- The plan for the child is adoption – local authority is no longer planning for the possibility of return to the birth family
- As soon as possible after coming into care, child is placed with approved adopters who have temporary approval to foster a named child (while waiting for formal authority to place, e.g. formal consent or placement order)
- Child is adopted by these adopters when legalities are finalised
- NB There are still some relinquished babies where formal consent is given after six weeks – some of these babies may be adopted via the "fostering for adoption" route

3. Concurrent planning (in baby adoptions)

- Child is removed from birth parents and taken into care
- A plan is made for assessment and rehabilitation so that child can return to birth parents
- At the same time, plans are made for the child to be adopted
- Child is placed with prospective adopter who is also an approved foster carer

Preparing to adopt

- Concurrency carers care for the child while social workers continue to work with the birth parents
- Concurrency carers take child to birth parent(s) for regular supervised contact sessions
- If return home proves unworkable, the child is adopted by concurrency carers
    - Only used in cases where return to birth parents is considered highly unlikely
    - Concurrency carers look after the child with a view to adopting the child but at the same time they understand that rehabilitation is also being explored and that there is a possibility the child will return home. Concurrency carers are required to balance their own wishes and desires with an acceptance of what is deemed to be best for the child.

In the conventional model of adoption, most children are taken into care and spend some time with foster carers before adoptive parents are found and the child is placed with them.

In the Adoption Action Plan published in 2012, the Government sought to promote practices aimed at placing children for adoption as early as possible with the carers who are likely to become their adoptive parents. Fostering for adoption and concurrent planning are routes through which this can be achieved.

Fostering for adoption and concurrent planning both aim to get the child into his adoptive family as early as possible. But because the child is placed with prospective adopters before the placement order is made, these routes require the adults – the prospective adopters – to take on some risk for the sake of reducing the risks to the child of multiple moves (e.g. from a foster placement to prospective adopters).

Statutory adoption guidance advises that the agency should discuss with the prospective adopter whether they may be interested in fostering a child for whom adoption is thought to be a likely outcome.

Unnecessary delay and moves are to be avoided if possible. However, it is not always clear straight away whether a child in care will ultimately need to be placed for adoption or will be able to return home or perhaps go to live with other relatives; a period of assessment is often necessary and this is in the child's best interests.

If adoption is the plan, the legal processes and family-finding can take some time.

Every move involves loss and disruption for the child, and risks damaging the child's development and ability to form attachments. If a child is going to need a new adoptive family, it is in the child's best interests to be placed with this family as early as possible so that he can begin to bond with his new parents.

However, if there is a chance – however small – that the birth mother (and possibly also the father) may be able to make the necessary changes to enable them to keep the child, they must be allowed to have a limited amount of time to show that they have done this and that they can look after him properly.

In concurrent planning, the baby (it is usually a baby) lives with the prospective adopters but spends a significant amount of time with the birth mother (and possibly father) – under

What is adoption?

supervision. Concurrent planning adopters have to be prepared to take the baby to spend some time with the birth parent(s) in a neutral venue such as a family centre – this might be for several hours, several times a week. During this period, the birth parents' parenting abilities and attempts at lifestyle changes (e.g. giving up drugs) are assessed.

Concurrent planning means that if these attempts fail the baby will not have to be moved again and can stay with the adopters. It allows the baby and the prospective adopters to begin bonding as early as possible.

With fostering for adoption, it is less likely that there will be any direct contact between the carers and with the birth parents but if contact is taking place for the child, social workers will need to assess whether it is appropriate for the carers to be involved.

With both fostering for adoption and concurrent planning, there is always going to be the option that the court may decide not to make a placement order. It is not at all easy for prospective adopters to look after and bond with a baby or child while having to accept the uncertainty and the risk, however small, that they may not be able to keep the child, and they will need to be well supported.

Show DVD clip

Show the DVD clip of two families talking about their adoption experiences.

Exercise

What we have to offer

- Explain to the group that even if someone has never had children of their own, they will have other relevant and valuable insights and experiences to bring to adoption. Stress that some participants may not yet realise the relevance of some of their experiences.

- Ask the group for examples of some of the varied life experiences people may have had which could help equip them to meet the needs of a child. The group may suggest, for instance: separation from people they love, bereavement, coming from a mixed heritage background, having looked after other people's children, having mentored a young person, having experience of parenting their own birth child. Write up their suggestions on the flip chart.

- Ask participants to divide into small groups and discuss what each of them brings to adoption. Tell them that you won't be asking them to share this with the larger group. Encourage them to make notes on the relevant page of their Workbook if they would like to do this.

Preparing to adopt

Presentation

What do we need in order to become adoptive parents?

Explain to the participants that at the end of Stage One they will have to decide whether they would like to proceed to Stage Two of the assessment process. Based on the information it has gathered during Stage One, the agency will make a decision on whether each participant can continue to Stage Two.

Explain that Stage Two involves assessment of their suitability as well as further, more intensive, preparation for the task of adoption; during the four months of Stage Two, these processes are run in parallel.

With the help of the following slides, briefly explain the scope of the Prospective Adopter's Report (PAR) and the checks, references and personal details that will be needed. Explain that the PAR is required by legislation and provides a comprehensive picture of prospective adopters and the experiences, skills and values they are bringing.

Try to demystify the idea of "adoptive parenting capacity".

SLIDE Introduction to assessment

Assessment is designed to enable you to:

- Understand your strengths
- Form a view about your capacity to care for/parent a child
- Explore your motivation for wanting to adopt
- Assess the stability and permanence of your relationship (for couples)
- Assess the robustness of your support network
- Identify areas for further development

SLIDE "Adoptive parenting capacity": what does it mean?

- Having realistic expectations about adoption
- Understanding the needs of adopted children
- Being able to respond to the needs of a child or children with a history of maltreatment, loss or trauma
- Being able to support and encourage a child's sense of identity and self-esteem (including if the child is from a different ethnic background)

What is adoption?

SLIDE Why do adopters have to be assessed?

- Because children who are being adopted need a secure base
- Many have experienced trauma
- They will all have suffered loss
- They may feel that the world is an unsafe place and adults cannot be trusted
- They may have come to expect rejection or punishment
- Their emotions, relationships and behaviour are all likely to be affected
- Adopters will need to demonstrate their capacity to respond to such children

Information for trainers

Some participants may openly wonder why prospective adopters need to undergo such a detailed assessment and "jump through hoops" in order to adopt a child when there are no such checks for those who conceive a child naturally. Hopefully, by the time they have completed the Stage One module *The Children* and the Stage Two modules, the answer to this question will have become clear to them. Meanwhile, explain that adoptive parenting makes particular demands on parents. These children need a "secure base" and adoptive parents need special qualities and skills to parent other people's children. Even where children are placed as babies, they will have particular lifelong needs in relation to understanding their identity and origins, and adopters will have to support them as they grow.

Exercise

What a child loses

Below, we provide the fictional story of a child's life from birth to adoption. In this exercise, group members represent all the key people in a child's life as various significant events unfold in the child's life story.

Give a "health warning" to the group as this may resonate with participants' own experiences of loss (their own personal history, etc.). Tell them that if anyone feels upset, they can leave the room and/or come and talk to you or the other trainer afterwards if they need to.

As you start to read out the story, hold a doll in your arms to represent the child, who is called Lexy. Then hand the doll to another person in the group as indicated in the story below – the doll is handed on from one person to another every time the child experiences a separation or loss.

Course participants are ascribed a role as the story is narrated, for example, birth mother,

Preparing to adopt

brother, sister, grandmother, grandfather, social worker, foster carer and so on. They do not have to speak but ask them to "sculpt" their feelings/emotions as the child/doll is passed around. In other words, their body language, the direction they are facing and so on should all indicate how they think their "character" would be feeling at any given time.

At the end of the story, course participants are asked to come out of their roles. You should discuss with the group how they felt about this exercise. Some of them may be feeling sad.

Ask the participant who took the role of "Sarah", the adopter, how she feels about all the broken relationships Lexy had experienced before she came to be adopted.

Ask "Sarah" how she feels about Mark, the brother left behind, and whether she would like her adopted daughters to be able to continue to see him occasionally.

Remind the group that some children in care experience even more changes and losses than Lexy did in the story.

Acknowledge how pleased everyone will be that Lexy and Jodie are finally getting a lovely "forever family" after so long. Then juxtapose this with all the losses that Lexy and Jodie will experience as a result of adoption as well as the losses of birth family and previous carers. Encourage the participants to reflect on the other losses that the girls may experience as a result of being adopted: people, teachers, familiar places such as their nursery and school, foster siblings, pets, school friends, activities, social groups and so on.

Finally, ask the group what they think Lexy and her sister need now, after all they have experienced. The response will probably be that the children need to find security and stability with their adopter, Sarah, who can help them recover.

This leads on to the following presentation about the "secure base model".

HANDOUT

Lexy's story

Lexy was born to 22-year-old Jade who had two older children, three-year-old Mark and two-year-old Jodie. *(Allocate the roles of Jade, Mark and Jodie to three of the participants and hand the doll to Jade.)*

Jade was separated from Andy, the father of Mark and Jodie. He had gone abroad and no one knew where he was. At the time she conceived Lexy, Jade was living in a squat, drinking and smoking a lot of cannabis and had multiple sexual partners so was not sure who Lexy's father was. Jade moved in with her parents during her pregnancy and she left most of the child care to her parents, Jim and Moira *(allocate the roles of Jim and Moira to two other participants)*. Jim and Moira tried to support her and the children as well as they could. Jade was not interested in looking after Lexy. *(Jade hands the doll to Moira and Jim.)*

What is adoption?

But when Lexy was seven months old, Jade met a new boyfriend, Jez *(allocate this role to a participant)*, and after a couple of months she moved in with him and took the children with her. *(Moira and Jim hand the doll to Jade and Jez; Mark and Jodie follow.)*

However, it soon became clear that Jez was a violent man and after six months Jade and the children moved into a women's refuge *(Jade, Mark and Jodie turn their back on Jez and step away from him)*. They were there for three months. At first Moira and Jim said they couldn't cope with having Jade and the children back, because of their own ill-health. But they relented and Jade and the children moved back, with Moira and Jim again providing much of the childcare. *(Jade hands the doll back to Moira and Jim.)*

When Lexy was two years old, Jim died suddenly. Moira was grief-stricken and became depressed and unable to look after the children. In addition, by this time her arthritis had got worse and she was unable to do the physical caring they needed. Jade was drinking heavily. She agreed that the children should be taken into care. *(Allocate the role of social worker to a participant; Moira and Jade hand the doll to the social worker.)*

The three children were fostered by short-term foster carers Hannah and John. *(Allocate the roles of Hannah and John. Social worker hands the doll to Hannah and John; Mark and Jodie follow.)*

Three months later Jade said she wanted the children back. She was asked to attend an assessment unit with the children for six weeks. *(Hannah and John hand the doll to Jade; Mark and Jodie follow.)* But in spite of Jade being offered support for her alcohol abuse, she was unable to stop drinking and provide the care the children needed. The local authority applied for a care order.

The children went to another set of foster carers, Sheila and Barry. *(Jade hands the doll to participants who have been allocated the roles of Sheila and Barry; Mark and Jodie follow.)* By now Mark was showing disturbed behaviour. Sheila and Barry found it extremely demanding to look after him. The children's social worker assessed their needs and it was decided that they needed to be adopted, but that Mark should be adopted separately from his sisters as he needed one-to-one care as the only child in an adoptive family.

When Lexy was three and Jodie was five, they were placed with Sarah for adoption. *(Sheila and Barry hand the doll to Sarah; Jodie follows, but Mark stays behind with Sheila and Barry.)*

Information for trainers

The story of Lexy also features in another module, in Stage Two, where it is used in a different way.

Preparing to adopt

Presentation

Providing a secure base for an adopted child

SLIDE What is a secure base?

A secure base is provided through a relationship with one or more sensitive and responsive attachment figures who meet the child's needs and to whom the child can turn as a safe haven, when upset or anxious.

(Schofield and Beek, 2014)

SLIDE Helping the child recover and building resilience

Components of a secure base (Schofield and Beek, 2014)

- Being available
- Responding sensitively
- Accepting the child
- Co-operative caregiving
- Promoting a sense of belonging

Tell the group that in a later module they will learn much more about the need to provide a secure base for adopted children and how to help them develop resilience.

Information for trainers

A secure base

When children develop trust in the availability and reliability of the relationship with their attachment figure(s), their anxiety is reduced and they can therefore explore and enjoy their world, safe in the knowledge that they can return to their secure base for help if needed. Schofield and Beek (2014) point out that the concept of a secure base is essential to our understanding of how children form relationships and how they develop. It links attachment and exploration, and provides the basis of a secure attachment. A securely attached child does not only seek comfort from an attachment figure, but by feeling safe to explore, develops confidence, competence and resilience.

What is adoption?

Presentation

The child's journey to adoption

Talk through the routes by which a child becomes looked after and potentially is placed for adoption (see Figures 1 and 2, pp 40–41), while the participants look at the same flowcharts in their Workbook.

Thus you will briefly describe the child's journey from being relinquished or taken into care, right through to matching, introductions, adoption placement and the adoption order.

Presentation by adopters and DVD clip

One or perhaps two adopters whom you have invited should address the group and talk about their experience of adopting a child. If you are able to have two adopters to speak, one of these should be someone who has been through the assessment process within the last year.

If it is not possible to invite any adopters to address the group, you may instead wish to show the clip from the DVD, which features a family with a birth daughter talking about adopting a little boy and a couple who talk about life with their adopted son.

Information for trainers

These personal accounts should be largely positive and emphasise the joys and pleasures of parenthood. They should not focus on the adoption process (which is covered in another module) but on life with an adopted child (or children).

If participants would like to read more about the experiences of adopters, refer them to BAAF's Our Story series and to the extracts that appear in their Workbook. BAAF's Our Story series includes a number of personal narratives by adopters or foster carers on their parenting experiences – visit www.baaf.org.uk/bookshop for more information.

The voice of the child and DVD clip

Remind participants of the first exercise, when they came up with words that came to mind about adoption for each of the letters in the word "adoption". Now show them this poem, which gives an adopted child's version of the same exercise. Alternatively, you could show the clip from the DVD, in which Chantelle reads out the poem, *ADOPTION*.

Preparing to adopt

Figure 1 **Routes by which a child becomes looked after and potentially is placed for adoption**

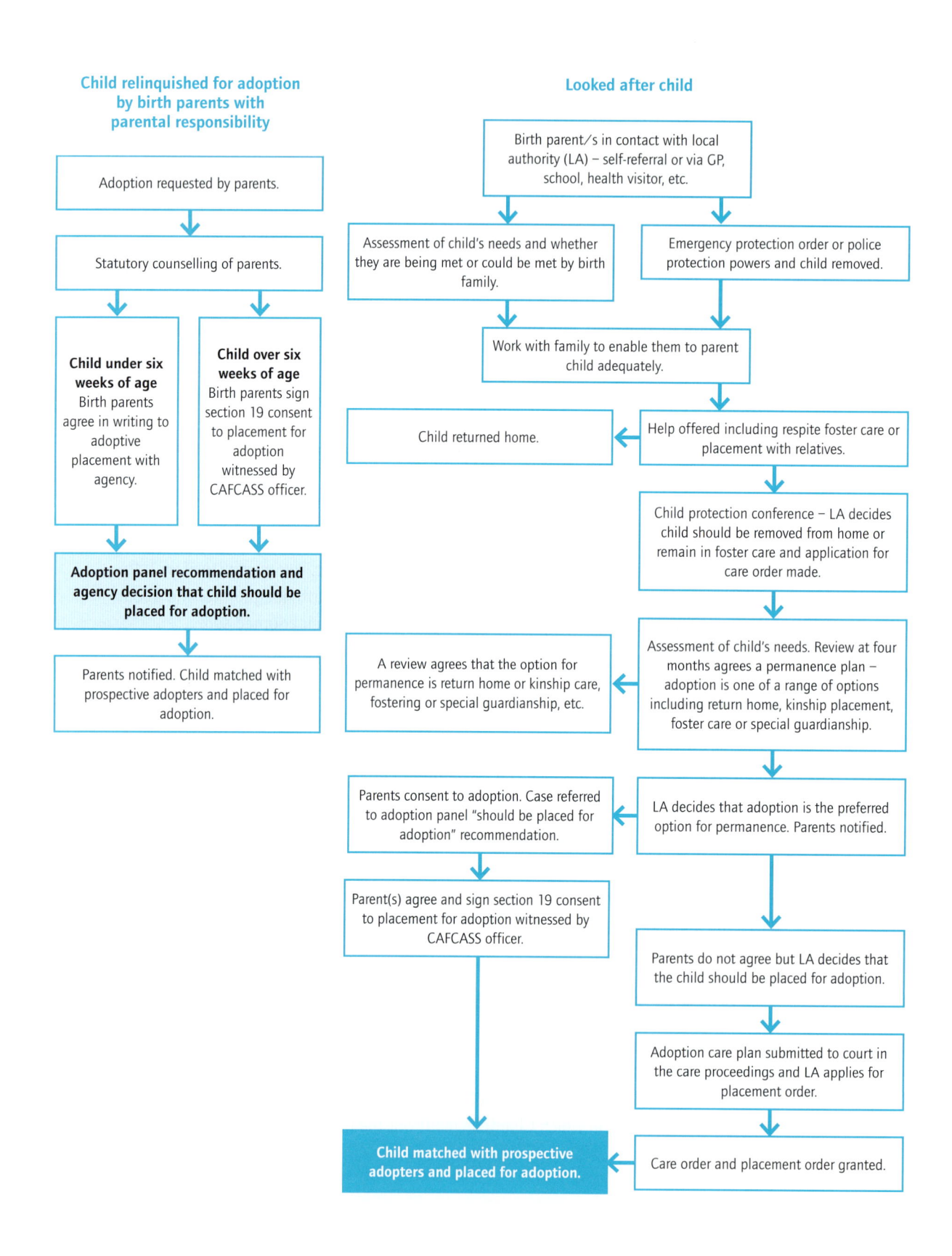

Child relinquished for adoption by birth parents with parental responsibility

- Adoption requested by parents.
- ↓
- Statutory counselling of parents.
- ↓

Child under six weeks of age
Birth parents agree in writing to adoptive placement with agency.

Child over six weeks of age
Birth parents sign section 19 consent to placement for adoption witnessed by CAFCASS officer.

↓

Adoption panel recommendation and agency decision that child should be placed for adoption.

↓

Parents notified. Child matched with prospective adopters and placed for adoption.

Looked after child

- Birth parent/s in contact with local authority (LA) – self-referral or via GP, school, health visitor, etc.

Branches to:
- Assessment of child's needs and whether they are being met or could be met by birth family.
- Emergency protection order or police protection powers and child removed.

↓

Work with family to enable them to parent child adequately.

↓

- Child returned home.
- Help offered including respite foster care or placement with relatives.

↓

Child protection conference – LA decides child should be removed from home or remain in foster care and application for care order made.

↓

Assessment of child's needs. Review at four months agrees a permanence plan – adoption is one of a range of options including return home, kinship placement, foster care or special guardianship.

↓

- A review agrees that the option for permanence is return home or kinship care, fostering or special guardianship, etc.
- LA decides that adoption is the preferred option for permanence. Parents notified.

↓

- Parents consent to adoption. Case referred to adoption panel "should be placed for adoption" recommendation.
- Parents do not agree but LA decides that the child should be placed for adoption.

↓

- Parent(s) agree and sign section 19 consent to placement for adoption witnessed by CAFCASS officer.
- Adoption care plan submitted to court in the care proceedings and LA applies for placement order.

↓

Child matched with prospective adopters and placed for adoption. ← Care order and placement order granted.

Reproduced (with amendments) from *Effective Adoption Panels*, 6th edn., BAAF, 2013.

What is adoption?

Figure 2 **The Adoption Planning Process in England and Wales**

For the child looked after in public care and following Core Assessment

Placement Order is granted by the court

↓

Adoption placement report is completed

↓

Adopters must agree to proceed

↓

**Match is taken to panel for recommendation
Followed by agency decision**
(The CPR/CAAR, the prospective adopters' report (PAR) and the adoption placement report are submitted to the panel.)

↓

Life Appreciation Day (optional)

↓

Adopters must confirm that they wish to proceed once they have had the agency proposals, which include elements of parental responsibility, in the Adoption Placement Plan

↓

Introduction planning meeting

↓

Meeting to review introductions

↓

Placement

↓

Review of adoption placement
(at one month, four months and beyond that at six-monthly intervals until an Order is made)

↓

Adoption application is made

↓

ADOPTION ORDER

Preparing to adopt

SLIDE *Adoption*, by Chantelle, aged 12

*A*ngry at birth parents

*D*aring to trust new family

*O*bedience is very hard

*P*atience is needed

*T*ime is a healer

I need to be helped

*O*dd feelings are flying

*N*o one can understand me

(In Harris, 2008, p 87)

To conclude

Tell the group that you hope they are starting to develop a deeper understanding of what adoption means, both for the child and for the adopters. There are many children desperately waiting for a family of their own. By adopting, people can experience the joys and rewards of having a family while giving a child (or children) love, stability and a new, brighter future.

You may wish to finish with the closing exercise on page 26 or another closing exercise of your choice.

Suggested reading for trainers

Department for Education (2013) *Statutory Guidance on Adoption* (Chapter 3)

Schofield G and Beek M (2006) *Attachment Handbook for Foster Care and Adoption*, London: BAAF

Simmonds J (2013) *Fostering for Adoption: Becoming a carer*, London: Coram and BAAF

References

Harris P (ed) (2008) *The Colours in Me: Writing and poetry by adopted children and young people*, London: BAAF

Neil Salter A (2013) *The Adopter's Handbook*, London: BAAF

Schofield G and Beek M (2014) *The Secure Base Model: Promoting attachment and resilience in foster care and adoption*, London: BAAF

MODULE 2

The children

Timing

This module is likely to take between two-and-a-half and three hours, not including any refreshment breaks.

Setting the scene

- Introduce yourself and explain your role in the agency. Explain to the group that the aim of this adoption preparation is to give them a realistic idea of the task ahead. It will also help them to decide whether adoption is something they want to do and are ready for.

- Remind the group where this session fits into your agency's training programme.

- Refer to housekeeping issues (e.g. fire escapes, toilets, timing of breaks and the time the session will end).

- Explain and outline the ground rules listed in the *Introduction* on page 17.

  For this module you will need:

- copies of the handouts (profiles and photographs, the quiz *Who are the children?* and quiz answers);

- a copy of *Be My Parent* newspaper.

Introductions/warm-up exercise

Choose one of the warm-up exercises listed on pp 24–26 to put the group at their ease and to get them to introduce themselves to each other.

Learning outcomes

SLIDE The children

This module aims to:

- explain why some children need to be adopted

- give you a better understanding of the kind of children who are waiting and their varied backgrounds

- explain how you can find out about children waiting to be adopted

Preparing to adopt

Exercise

Meet some children

Below, we provide eight case studies based on real children (including sibling groups). Some of these case studies are drawn from BAAF's Parenting Matters series, which looks at a number of health needs and conditions. The case studies are in two parts: a brief profile describing a child in care, and a follow-up account of what happened to the child after he/she was adopted.

Put copies of the brief profiles of children (available on the CD-ROM to print out) around the room on several tables and ask participants to go round the tables and read all the profiles in turn. Ask them to consider, while reading each profile, whether they might be able to think about adopting a child with a similar background and/or similar difficulties.

In the second part of the exercise, participants hear "what happened next" in each case. Summarise or read out the follow-up accounts to explain what happened next. For variety, you could ask for volunteers from the group to read them out.

At the end, discuss with the group their thoughts on these outcomes. At the beginning of the exercise you asked them to think about whether they might have felt able to consider adopting a child or children like these. How does it feel to hear what happened to the children next?

Brief profiles of the children

Thomas and Christopher

Twins Thomas and Christopher were born 10 weeks early to a mother who misused drugs. Both babies stayed in hospital for six weeks to manage their drug withdrawal symptoms. Christopher had some seizures related to drug withdrawal. They were slow to establish a feeding and sleeping routine.

The babies went straight from hospital to foster care. Christopher has a mild spastic diplegia, which means the muscles on his inner thighs are very tense. Thomas has some speech delay. At the age of two, both boys are underweight and their understanding of speech is around the level of a one-year-old. Christopher is unsteady on his feet and screams a lot. Thomas is clingy towards his foster carer and has poor eye contact.

The children

Sophie, Ben and Lucy

Sophie, Ben and Lucy were born to birth parents who both had learning difficulties. The children witnessed considerable violence and were neglected.

Sophie, aged four, is considered by her foster carers to be a difficult child. She shows no affection and has severe tantrums. She doesn't know how to play. All she really wants to do is watch television.

Ben, at nearly three, is still not talking. He covers his head at the sound of any loud noise and hides when things don't go his way.

Lucy, aged nearly one, is lively and everyone adores her. She is most content when playing with water and "cleaning". She struggles with speech, but smiles at everyone.

Alisha

Six-year-old Alisha was neglected by her birth parents. She has been with her foster carers for several years and is very attached to them, but they are unable to keep her permanently. Her foster carers and social workers recognise that it will be painful for her to leave them if she ever finds an adoptive family. Alisha is of normal intelligence but is behind at school.

Adam and James

Adam and James are aged one and four. James is at a mainstream school. At times he can become very angry. His younger brother, Adam, is developmentally delayed but improving now that he is in foster care. Their story is one of severe neglect and physical abuse in a dysfunctional family. The plan is for the boys to be adopted together.

Rani

Rani is a four-week-old baby who is developing well. Her parents have both been diagnosed with schizophrenia. They are unable to care for her at present and are unlikely to be able to do so in the future.

Preparing to adopt

Daniel

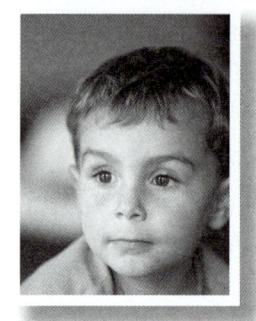

Daniel, aged two, was born in the UK to parents who had come here from Eastern Europe. His father is now in prison and his mother is in a relationship with another man. She is rejecting Daniel and has made it clear she does not want to care for him any longer. She has no family to support her or to look after Daniel.

Leon

Five-year-old Leon is a healthy, active African-Caribbean boy. He is living with foster carers and attending a Baptist church. He has been in foster care for some time and wants to find a "forever family".

Jamie

Jamie is a six-month-old baby who has cerebral palsy and needs to be fed through a tube. His birth parents are unable to care for him.

Follow-up accounts of what happened to the children

Thomas and Christopher

Twins Thomas and Christopher were adopted at age two. They made remarkable progress in the early months after their adoption but it was still obvious that they were developmentally delayed. They also frequently bit each other, their adoptive mother and other children.

Both boys turned out to be very musical. Going to a music group with them, says their adoptive mother, 'enabled me to see my children properly for the first time and to really recognise that despite the drug-abusing background and prematurity, there were two bright little boys in there just trying to find the right way out'.

The children

Christopher did well at school but Thomas was unhappy. Eventually Thomas was diagnosed as autistic. 'He has made slow but steady and amazing progress with a Statement of Special Needs and one-to-one support. He is on the gifted and talented register for art and is clearly an intelligent little boy.'

Three years after the twins were adopted, their birth mother had another baby, Richard, who joined his brothers in their adoptive family when he was 12 months old. Although Richard was tiny and remains very small for his age, he is a bright and able child.

Thomas and Christopher have additional needs. Christopher wears splints on his feet and legs to help with his walking; his adoptive parents believe he has mild cerebral palsy. Thomas is autistic and still wets his pants during the day. Their adoptive parents still consider the boys vulnerable and Christopher in particular is easily led. But all three of the boys have positive personalities and charm everyone they meet.

(Adapted from Forrester, 2012)

Sophie, Ben and Lucy

In the years after their adoption, the children became increasingly affectionate towards their adoptive parents and each other. However, they each had their difficulties. When there was not enough structure (e.g. at school playtimes) they could not cope, either emotionally or behaviourally.

Sophie continued to have tantrums. 'We gradually accepted that, like her birth parents, Sophie had learning difficulties and that these impacted on her understanding and hence her behaviour...we accepted Sophie for who she was, realising that with her level of understanding, life was a daily challenge. As soon as we appreciated her difficulties, we were much more able to see and rejoice when we saw progress,' says her adoptive mother.

As Ben grew older, his behaviour was often hard to deal with – he stole from family and friends, told lies, smashed things up when he got angry. His adoptive parents worked out what would help him to manage his feelings and behaviour and did whatever they could to increase his self-esteem and build a healthy relationship with him. Gradually he has developed the ability to regulate his emotions and behaviours. Ben is now 14. Because of his difficulty in coping with secondary school his adopters took the decision to home-school him, which has been successful and he is now much happier.

Lucy, it turned out, had attention deficit hyperactivity disorder (ADHD) and autistic spectrum disorder, so she has difficulty in school and with making friendships.

The children's birth mother subsequently had two more children, Harry and Daniel, who eventually also joined the family. Although Harry and Daniel were of school age by then, all the children quickly gelled together.

At first Harry ate everything he could get his hands on, whether he was hungry or not, and he was extremely destructive. But he is doing much better now.

Daniel, the youngest, was wary at first and withdrew from physical contact, but as time went

Preparing to adopt

on he became a very affectionate child. He enjoys school and makes friends easily. He does not have the emotional and behavioural difficulties of his brothers and sisters.

Reflecting on their experiences and how far the children have come, their adoptive mother concludes: 'You have to have lived through it to understand how difficult life has been but what had so often seemed impossible had actually happened – we were definitely a happy, if not always a conventional, family.'

(Adapted from Hughes, 2012)

Alisha

Alisha was adopted by Julia, a single woman who had adopted another girl, Nicky, four years earlier. Julia had decided, after her partner had died, that she wanted to adopt – she didn't want to have another relationship just for the sake of having children. Adopting Nicky, as a single parent, had required perseverance, but has been a success. Julia was keen to adopt a second child and Nicky wanted a sister; Julia first saw Alisha in the family-finding newspaper *Be My Parent*.

At first Alisha missed her foster family and repeatedly told Julia: 'I love Maggie a lot more than I love you'. But things have moved on and Alisha talks less about her foster mum and dad as she becomes more settled. 'Alisha now loves going to school and has caught up. She is very stable, loving and attached', says Julia, and adds that the two sisters have developed a good relationship.

(Adapted from Sturge-Moore, 2005)

Adam and James

Adam and James were adopted by Jim and Helen, a couple who decided to adopt after unsuccessful infertility treatment. Adam was referred to several different clinics and to a playgroup for children with disabilities. He was a passive child who avoided eye contact and did not speak. James struggled with school and was only really happy when playing with toy cars, putting them in huge traffic jams all in the right order. Adam's lack of eye contact, repetitive play and delayed speech led to a diagnosis of autism. As Helen learned more about autism, she realised that James also showed signs of the condition. He was finally diagnosed with autism spectrum disorder at seven years old.

Both boys now attend special needs schools, where they are thriving. Adam can now talk, read, write and add up. He needs a lot of encouragement and simple instructions. Echolalia (repeating words without understanding the meaning) features high in his autism. James's autistic tendencies are less obvious – he has some mild echolalia and repetitive behaviours and his understanding of language is poor. He is fascinated by learning about trains, buses and bus routes, maps and football stadiums.

Everyday life with children on the autistic spectrum can be tiring and hard work. But it can also be rewarding, say Jim and Helen. Despite thinking, before they adopted, that they would not be able to accept a child with autism: 'We love them unconditionally and we know they love us. It is not true that autistic children cannot love you or show you affection. They just sometimes show you in a different way.'

(Adapted from Carter, 2013)

Rani

Rani was placed under a "fostering to adopt" arrangement with Meera and Aadi, who have come to adoption because of infertility. They were understandably anxious about the possibility of losing Rani if the court were to decide that she should return to her parents. They talked all this through with their social worker and they also discussed the implications of her parents' mental illness with the agency's medical adviser. But they very much wanted to adopt a baby and decided the risk was small and they were prepared to take it. So Rani went to live with them and after four quite stressful months of waiting, the placement order was granted and they were matched as an adoptive placement. Rani continues to develop well. Meera and Aadi are delighted with their little girl.

Daniel

Daniel went into foster care at two and was placed with adoptive parents, Charlie and Jane, six months later. He had made good progress in his foster family. He took some time to settle with his adoptive parents but over time he began to trust them and he is now a bright, happy child who is doing well.

Leon

Leon is being permanently fostered in an African-Caribbean family: Ken and Polly and their four birth daughters, aged from nine to 21, not to mention their large extended family who all live nearby. They are committed to keeping him permanently. 'We felt we could help a black child develop a strong sense of himself and give him the things he missed out on,' says Polly. The couple had been approved to become long-term foster carers and found Leon through the family-finding paper *Be My Parent*. When Leon first moved in, she says, 'he was very excited, but there were moments of sadness too, when he missed his previous carers. Once he knew that this was okay and he could talk about them, he started to settle. He's cheeky, amusing, vulnerable and, yes, naughty – all a good sign that he is comfortable...We know we did the right thing.'

(Adapted from Sturge-Moore, 2005)

Jamie

Jamie was adopted by Rosie and Paul, a couple with three older birth children. Their fourth child, a daughter, was born with severe disabilities and had died at the age of 18 months. Through their experience with their daughter, they had become aware of the children with

Preparing to adopt

disabilities left in hospital because their parents found it too difficult to cope. They had decided they would like to adopt a child with disabilities.

As Jamie grew older, he needed to use a wheelchair and the family received support to pay for alterations to their house – a ramp, a downstairs shower room, and turning the dining room into a bedroom. Jamie no longer needs to be fed through a tube.

As Rosie and Paul became more confident in parenting Jamie, they decided to adopt another child with a disability. Steven, who also has cerebral palsy and uses a wheelchair, joined the family. Steven is a year older than Jamie. Both boys have flourished and have lots of friends. They attend mainstream school – their school has a lift and wide corridors for good wheelchair access. Rosie says: 'You see a huge shift in the children when they start feeling secure and are able to say: "This is my mum, my dad, my room, my bed, my class, my teacher".'

(Adapted from Sturge-Moore, 2005)

Information for trainers

These case studies may throw up some new considerations for members of the group. Some participants may never have considered the possibility of another child being born to the birth mother after a child or children had already been adopted. The case studies also illustrate the fact that, with many children who are adopted at an early age, it's impossible to predict with accuracy how they will develop or whether their difficulties will resolve or worsen.

The case study for Leon raises questions about what happens to children when adopters cannot be found – is long-term fostering a good outcome for a five-year-old? What are the disadvantages? The Government is expecting that the search would be widened to include families who would not reflect a child's ethnicity but his age and gender may still put him at a disadvantage.

A number of these case studies are genuine cases including actual quotes from adopters, while others are "composite" case studies; all the corresponding photos provided are "posed by models".

Alternatively, you could use profiles of children for whom your agency is actually looking for families, or for whom it has found families. If using your own profiles, you should aim to represent the full range of children both locally and nationally who need families, e.g. sibling groups (at least two groups); a baby born to a substance-abusing mother; a "fostering to adopt" scenario; a child of Eastern European birth parents; an older child; a child with significant impairments/disability; a child from a minority ethnic or mixed heritage background.

If focusing on children from your own agency who are still awaiting adoption, you can speculate about what might happen, rather than reading out a follow-up account.

The children

SLIDE Why do children need adoptive families?

- Reasons why children may come into care
- How will these impact on planning for permanence?

Presentation/discussion

Why do children need adoptive families?

- Referring back to the case studies from the earlier exercise, ask participants to suggest some general reasons why children may need adoption. Write their answers on the flip chart.
- Discuss the varied reasons for children coming into care and the impact these reasons have on planning for permanence.
- Explain that in some cases there may be a member of the child's wider family or close family friend who could offer a permanent home for the child. If there is no one suitable or willing, social workers will look for an adoptive family.
- Refer to "fostering to adopt" and concurrent planning.

Information for trainers

Ensure that participants understand that not all the children in the care system need adoption – many children will eventually be able to return home.

If participants wonder why adoption can sometimes take so long, explain that often the situation is uncertain – social workers may want to ascertain whether the birth parents could be supported to look after their children; they will also check out any potential alternative carers among family members. The legal processes also take time.

Fostering for adoption and concurrent planning are covered more fully in the module *What is adoption?* (see pp 31–33) but you may need to briefly explain these terms to any members of the group who have not already completed that particular module.

Preparing to adopt

Presentation

Characteristics of children needing adoption

Give each participant a copy of the quiz, in which the questions relate to numbers and types of children awaiting adoption nationally. Ask them to complete the quiz individually.

HANDOUT

Quiz: Who are the children?

1. The number of children in care in the UK has increased over the last five years.

   True ☐   False ☐

2. The number of children adopted from care in the UK has increased over the last five years.

   True ☐   False ☐

3. Children over 10 years old are never adopted.

   True ☐   False ☐

4. There are no infants or toddlers that need adoption.

   True ☐   False ☐

5. Most children adopted from care have suffered abuse or neglect.

   True ☐   False ☐

6. There are more boys needing adoption than there are girls.

   True ☐   False ☐

7. Half the children placed for adoption have one or more impairments or health conditions.

   True ☐   False ☐

8. Most children placed for adoption no longer have any contact with their birth family.

   True ☐   False ☐

9. Most children adopted from care are white, of English, Scottish, Welsh or Northern Irish descent.

   True ☐   False ☐

10. Children in large sibling groups are generally split and sent to different families.

    True ☐   False ☐

11. Children who are placed for adoption will quickly get over their early adverse experiences.

    True ☐   False ☐

The children

Give the handout below and go through the answers.

NB The figures are correct at the time of writing; in future years, you will need to update these figures.

HANDOUT

Who are the children?

1. **The number of children in care in the UK has increased over the last five years.**

   True. The number of looked after children has increased steadily over the last five years. In the year ending 31 March 2009, there were over 83,000 children in care, and in the year ending 31 March 2013, there were almost 93,000.

2. **The number of children adopted from care in the UK has increased over the last five years.**

   True. Although there have been shifts upwards and downwards over the last five years, the number of children adopted from care increased from around 3,800 in the year ending 31 March 2009 to around 4,600 in the year ending 31 March 2013.

3. **Children over 10 years old are never adopted.**

   False. Although the numbers remain small, some children of 10 and above are adopted. (Some of these are likely to be part of sibling groups containing younger siblings.)

4. **There are no infants or toddlers that need adoption.**

   False. There are a small number of babies and toddlers who need adoption.

   Note to trainer

   It is hard to be precise because the figures are so low and not available in all cases, and ages 1–5 tend to be grouped together. For England, here is the pattern of children in those two categories:

Year	2009	2010	2011	2012	2013
Under 1 year	80	70	60	80	90
1 to 4	2,380	2,260	2,210	2,570	2,960

Preparing to adopt

5. **Most children adopted from care have suffered abuse or neglect.**

   True. Around 70 per cent of children adopted have been taken into care because they have suffered neglect and/or some form of abuse – emotional, physical or sexual.

   (It is difficult to give accurate figures. For England, it is around 70 per cent, but this is the category of need at the point of being taken into care, not the total number of children who are in care/being adopted who have experienced neglect or abuse.)

6. **There are more boys needing adoption than there are girls.**

   False. There are roughly equal proportions of boys and girls needing adoption.

7. **Half the children placed for adoption have one or more impairments or health conditions.**

   We don't know. There are no clear statistics available on disability. A significant minority of children featured in BAAF's family-finding service *Be My Parent* or referred to the Adoption Register do have some form of disability or impairment, but these children are generally those for whom it is harder to find a family, and so we cannot obtain a national picture. Also, it is worth remembering that, although a child may present with a particular condition in their early years, it can be possible to minimise its effects.

8. **Most children placed for adoption no longer have any contact with their birth family.**

   False. Although no figures are available, most children placed in recent years would have at least some form of indirect contact with some members of their birth family.

9. **Most children adopted from care are white, of English, Scottish, Welsh or Northern Irish descent.**

   True. However, black children and those of mixed ethnicity are over-represented among children in the care system, compared with the percentage of black and minority ethnic children in the general population.

10. **Children in large sibling groups are generally split and sent to different families.**

    It largely depends on how the siblings in the group function together and whether there are families available who could take on a sibling group. Where possible, siblings are placed together unless there are factors that clearly indicate that this would not be beneficial to the children. However, there is a shortage of adopters prepared to take sibling groups so, sadly, groups of siblings sometimes have to be split up (e.g. a large group may be split into pairs) because this gives them a better chance of finding adoptive parents. Where

The children

siblings are placed separately, it is important that there are clear plans in place for them to stay in contact with each other.

11. **Children who are placed for adoption will quickly get over their early adverse experiences.**

    This will depend on the individual child. Although the stability and security of a loving family will certainly help children to recover faster than they might otherwise, sometimes it can take a long time for children to begin to trust adults and develop an attachment to their adoptive parents. In some cases, therapeutic help is required.

Presentation

The children needing adoption

These case studies and facts and figures may have acted as a reality check for some people in the group. Discuss this with the group. Explore how easy or difficult they think it will be for them to let go of their "dream child".

Note to trainers

Acknowledge that some of the participants may be feeling disappointed as it becomes clear that, if they go on to adopt, their child is unlikely to be the "dream child" they may have been picturing. Given time, most prospective adopters will be able to come to terms with the probabilities and to change their expectations about the child or children they might adopt. Some may eventually decide that they would be able to take on a child with a disability or a sibling group, for example.

Move the discussion on to the profile of children locally who need adoptive placements. Talk about the features of children your local authority or agency needs to place – for instance, are many of them in sibling groups, or are most from a particular ethnic group? If possible, also describe some specific children or sibling groups waiting for adoption and talk about their personalities and what they enjoy doing.

Outline the Government's and your agency's positions on placing children with adopters of a different ethnicity from that of the child.

The Department for Education has said that social workers placing children should not hold out for the "perfect" ethnic match and that children should be placed within a reasonable time-scale rather than waiting for a long time to find an ethnic match. Explain that if any of the group do go on to enquire about being matched with a child of a different ethnicity, they will need to demonstrate that they can meet the child's ethnicity and identity needs.

Preparing to adopt

SLIDE Ethnicity: some factors to consider

- Children awaiting adoption have increasingly complex ethnic backgrounds.
- This can make finding an ethnic match difficult.
- Meeting ethnicity and identity needs is essential for a child's healthy emotional development.
- In a transracial placement this requires conscious thought and effort.
- Transracial placements = adoption is more "public".
- Children who stand out as different from their adoptive families will have to cope with attention and questions from others.
- Diverse school, neighbourhood and friends of similar ethnic background all help.

SLIDE Adopters have important responsibilities to:

- celebrate difference and show they value the child's heritage and culture
- support the child's ethnic identity and self-esteem
- provide opportunities for the child to engage with his culture, religion and language
- understand the impact of subtle and overt racism in society
- avoid culturally insensitive responses and behaviours
- empathise with the child's experience
- challenge racism and help the child learn to tackle racism
- help the child to develop resilience
- provide positive role models who reflect the child's heritage

Information for trainers

The slides above and information below are drawn from a training pack called *Supporting Black and Minority Ethnic Adopted Children*, produced by the Post-Adoption Centre with Talawa.

Meeting ethnicity and identity needs forms an essential component in a child's overall development, and will actively promote their ability to develop secure attachments within their new adoptive family network. Where the adopter(s) may not be in a position to meet these needs directly themselves, their first task must be to openly recognise and value their child's racial and ethnic heritage. Secondly, they must help their child build or maintain links which positively reinforce the child's heritage; modelling this for their child in their own relationships with adults reflecting their child's background. Where this is achieved the child will feel valued for who they are and, therefore, will be free to develop secure attachments within their new families.

(Post-Adoption Centre/Talawa, 2008)

So there are specific tasks for adopters in transracial/transcultural placements; they need to give conscious thought to the way they will meet the child's cultural and identity needs.

SLIDE What might the child have experienced before adoption?

- Stereotyping, discrimination, racism and/or racial abuse
- Racism within the family of origin may have affected the child's self-esteem
- Black child in predominantly white family may have "white" self-image

Information for trainers

The child may have a birth father of a different ethnicity from the birth mother and all her other children.

Two or more siblings being adopted may have fathers of different ethnicities.

Racism within the family of origin: children may have been given either more or less preferential treatment based on their skin colour, reflecting racist attitudes outside the family or within the extended family. Adults around the child may have failed to challenge, or have colluded with, racist/discriminatory behaviour between siblings.

SLIDE Siblings and sibling relationships

- There is a range of sibling and sibling-type relationships – step-siblings, half-siblings and children brought up in the same household may consider each other as siblings
- Sibling relationships are different from other relationships – uninhibited, individualised, intimate
- Close long-term relationships – often our longest lifetime relationships

SLIDE Lifetime implications of separating siblings

Siblings suffer a loss when they are separated; they miss out on forming a close bond and sharing their childhood years. They also lose:

Preparing to adopt

- *a lifelong relationship*
- *support in adversity*
- *a shared history*
- *sense of kinship*
- *continuity and rootedness*
- *sources of knowledge about family*
- *resources for identity-building*

(Cairns and Fursland, 2008, p 53)

SLIDE Siblings – together or apart?

The aim is to keep them together if possible. However:

- Shortage of adopters for sibling groups – they may have to be split to find families
- If large group can't be placed together, may be placed singly or in twos
- Separated siblings likely to benefit from continued contact (e.g. between adoptive families)
- Contact can be either face-to-face or through letterbox exchange
- Contact may reduce anxiety, allow continuity of bond, shared positive memories
- Contact allows better awareness of birth family identity
- Every sibling relationship is unique – benefits and drawbacks of contact in every case
- Separated siblings who have not been able to maintain contact may search for and find one another in later life – perhaps when they are teenagers, using Facebook?

Note to trainers

Tell participants that social networking issues and unmediated contact via Facebook will be covered in the later module *Telling, contact and social networking*.

Where face-to-face contact is not possible, creative ways of maintaining contact can be considered – Skype, DVD exchange and so on.

SLIDE Separation from birth siblings at home

Separating a child from siblings who remain at home is thought to be a significant risk factor in making a secure permanent placement.

The children

For a child, it is doubly difficult to understand why you must leave your family when others remain behind, and the resulting trauma and confusion can destabilise a new placement. A disabled child may be especially prone to being separated in this way.

(Cousins, 2011)

SLIDE Sometimes it is safer to place siblings separately when:

- relationships between siblings are poor, hostile or exploitative
- behaviour between siblings is highly sexualised
- other continuing dysfunctional patterns of behaviour exist
- they have incompatible needs
- there is chronic scapegoating
- one child's needs make it impossible to find adopters to take all siblings together

SLIDE Children with disabilities

- Children with disabilities (learning difficulties/physical disabilities) may suffer discrimination, stigma, being marginalised
- Being "different" may lead to rejection and isolation from peers
- This can cause them to have negative feelings about themselves and low self-esteem
- Child may have difficulty expressing him/herself
- Children with a disability are more likely to be victims of abuse
(Department for Education, 2010)

SLIDE Some uncomfortable truths

- The older children get, the less likely they are to find an adoptive family
- Disabled children are at particular risk of being split up from brothers and sisters (to increase the chances of the others being adopted?)
- For some children, e.g. those with profound disabilities, no adopters can be found
- Full details about child's history, health, etc. are not always known
- Even if there is no indication that the child has been sexually abused, any child may disclose sexual abuse at any time after placement

Preparing to adopt

Information for trainers

Disabled children may be at particular risk of being split up from their siblings, as there is a belief that this gives the other children a better chance of being adopted. When this happens, it sends a disturbing message to the children.

Show DVD clip

Show the clip from the DVD which features three children talking about their adoption – *Three stories: one family.*

Presentation

'When can we see the children?'

Suggest to participants that letting go of their "dream child" will be easier once they start to find out about and relate to "real" children who are waiting to find adoptive families.

Explain that agencies have a duty to set out a matching plan with adopters once they are approved, which states how they and the adopters will search for an appropriate match.

The rest of this presentation should explain the various ways in which prospective adopters can find out about or meet "real" children.

Some of the things you can tell them about will be specific to your agency or to your adoption consortium, for example, if you hold adoption exchange events. Others are more general. Below are some examples.

SLIDE Adoption Activity Days

Note to trainers

Adoption Activity Days – originally piloted in the East Midlands by BAAF and now offered across England – are now included in the Government's adoption reform agenda. These activity days (often based around a theme e.g. circus, pirates, Disney, etc) provide an opportunity for prospective adopters to meet, play with and talk to some children who they would otherwise only read about or see in a photograph or DVD clip. Prospective adopters who are already approved or who have a panel date within three months can go along to these events where children who need families are brought along by their foster carers and social worker for a fun day of face-painting, crafts and play.

The children

Show DVD clip

Show the clips from the DVD which show an introduction to Adoption Activity Days and scenes from an actual Adoption Activity Day.

SLIDE *Be My Parent* website

Note to trainers

You could also have a copy of the *Be My Parent* newspaper to show to the group or show it online (www.bemyparent.org.uk). If your venue has no internet access, ensure that you have a copy of the newspaper instead. Even though participants are a long way from being approved as adopters, being able to view profiles and find out more about the kind of children needing adoption are likely to be helpful and motivating for them.

Be My Parent is one of BAAF's family-finding services. Local authorities can refer children to the service if they are unable to find a local adoptive family for them. *Be My Parent* publishes profiles and photographs of children waiting for adoption, in both a monthly newspaper and a secure online service. Anyone may visit the website and look at some limited profiles of children who need families. To view fuller profiles and more children, you have to register with *Be My Parent* and pay a subscription. There are also useful articles and information on adoption.

Even if adopters are not yet approved, or even being assessed, if they see a child for whom they think they are the right parent(s), they can contact the child's social worker to make an enquiry and find out more.

The cost of subscription varies – at the time of writing it costs £18.75 for three issues of the *Be My Parent* newspaper only; £30 for three issues plus three months' full access to the website. A year's subscription to the newspaper only is £52.50, while for both newspaper and web it is £87. Check www.bemyparent.org.uk for up-to-date information.

Show DVD clip

Show the clip about *Be My Parent*. Note: This is from a short film made in 2008 but much of it still stands.

Preparing to adopt

SLIDE Children Who Wait

Note to trainers

Adoption UK's family-finding service, *Children Who Wait*, is a secure online tool and a printed publication that features profiles of children waiting for adoption, including information on their backgrounds and needs, and in some cases online video content. Prospective adopters and their social workers can access *Children Who Wait* by joining Adoption UK; the service enables them to contact the child's (or children's) social worker directly.

The cost of membership and subscription varies – at the time of writing it is £74 if paid by direct debit (£30 for those on a low income) – see www.adoptionuk.org.uk for information.

Adoption UK also runs social and other events in different areas – you may be able to organise a representative to come and talk to the group about what is available in their area.

SLIDE Adoption exchange events

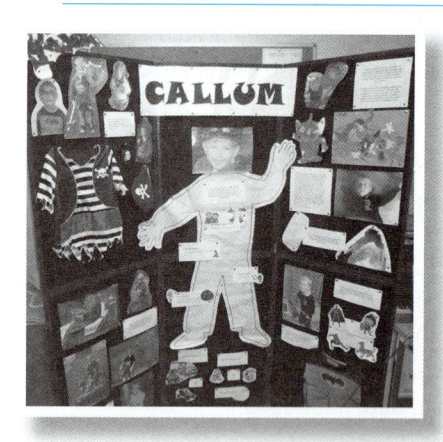

Note to trainers

Many local authority and voluntary adoption agencies and consortia join together to run "adoption exchange events". The Adoption Register also runs national adoption exchange events and sends along representatives to local events.

The agencies (and the Adoption Register) bring details, photographs and film clips of the children for whom they are looking for suitable families.

Adopters who have been approved can come along and find out more about the available children and may be able to chat to the children's social workers and register their interest.

SLIDE The Adoption Register for England

- A database of information about adopters and children who are waiting

The children

- The aim is to find suitable adopters for children wherever they live
- Children have not been found a family locally
- Agencies may refer adopters as soon as they have been approved
- Agencies *must* refer adopters to the Register three months after approval
- The Adoption Register for Wales was established in 2014.

Information for trainers

The Adoption Register works with adoption agencies and adoption consortia to make sure that all children and families have the best chance of finding a suitable match. Its main purpose is to find adoptive homes for those children for whom local authorities cannot find a home locally. The Adoption Register is operated by BAAF on behalf of the Department for Education. Wales has its own Adoption Register as of 2014.

Agencies can refer adopters to the Adoption Register as soon as they have been approved by the agency and will usually do this if it seems unlikely that the adopters will be matched quickly with a suitable child in their own region. Agencies must refer adopters to the Adoption Register three months after they have been approved if there is not a match with an identified child being actively pursued. Adopters can also self-refer three months after they have been approved. Agencies that are referring adopters must have the adopters' consent first.

At the time of writing, the Government is looking at how the Register can be made more accessible for adopters. You should explain any changes that have been introduced.

Show DVD clip

Show the DVD clip about the Adoption Register and Exchange Days.

Local consortia

You may also wish to refer to how your local adoption consortium works, if you have one, and explain when adopters will be referred to the consortium.

To conclude

Summarise for the group the message you would like them to take away from this module. It may go something like this:

Now you have learned more about the children who are waiting, you may have had to revise your thoughts about the kind of child you will be able to adopt. Some people may be feeling a little disappointed or daunted. Yes, there are some babies and toddlers who need adoption, but there are many older children. Some children, young or old, may have medical conditions, disabilities or problems stemming from early experiences. Some children who

Preparing to adopt

wait longest are in sibling groups, and need to be adopted together.

You may be unsure about adopting an older child, a sibling group or a child with special needs or a disability. Sometimes, though, prospective adopters meet a child they wouldn't have expected to be able to connect with and they find that there is something which draws them to that child, something which instinctively makes them feel that this child is the one for them. There will also be careful consideration in the assessment to make sure this is the right thing for them.

As you have read in the case studies and seen in the DVD clips, it can be a wonderful experience to provide a loving home and family for children who would otherwise wait for a long time.

You will learn more about the available children later in the process. For now, all you need to keep in mind is that, if you do go ahead, there is a child (or children!) out there waiting for you.

End the session with the closing exercise on page 26 or another of your choice.

Suggested reading for trainers

Argent H (2008) *Ten Top Tips for Placing Siblings*, London: BAAF

Cousins J (2011) *Ten Top Tips for Making Matches*, London: BAAF

Saunders H, Selwyn J with Fursland E (2013) *Placing Large Sibling Groups for Adoption*, London: BAAF

Also see BAAF's *Parenting Matters* series, various authors.

References

Cairns K and Fursland E (2008) 'Family ties' in *Building Identity*, London: BAAF/Akamas

Carter P (2013) *Parenting a Child with Autism Spectrum Disorder*, London: BAAF

Cousins J (2011) *Ten Top Tips for Making Matches*, London: BAAF

Department for Education (2010) 'Abuse of disabled children', in *Working Together to Safeguard Children*, London: DfE

Department for Education (2012) *An Action Plan for Adoption: Tackling delay*, London: DfE

Forrester D (2012) *Parenting a Child Affected by Parental Substance Misuse*, London: BAAF

Hughes D (2012) *Parenting a Child with Emotional and Behavioural Difficulties*, London: BAAF

Post-Adoption Centre/Talawa (2008) *Supporting Black and Minority Ethnic Adopted Children: Attachment and race – a training resource pack*, London: Post-Adoption Centre

Sturge-Moore L (ed) (2005) *Could you be my Parent? Adoption and fostering stories*, London: BAAF

MODULE 3

The adoption process

Timing

This module will take approximately two-and-a-half hours, not including a refreshment break. With a larger group it is likely to take longer.

Setting the scene

- Introduce yourself and explain your role in the agency. Explain to the group that the aim of this adoption preparation is to give them a realistic idea of the task ahead. It will also help them to decide whether adoption is something they want to do and are ready for.

- Remind the group how this module fits in with the training programme at your agency.

- Refer to housekeeping issues (e.g. fire escapes, toilets, timing of breaks and the time the session will end).

- Explain and outline the ground rules listed in the *Introduction* on page 17.

For this module you will need:

- some large sheets of paper and several pairs of scissors and rolls of sticky tape for the exercise *What is adoption like for a child?*;

- copies of the Adoption Passport (which you can print from the First4Adoption website) to give to all participants;

- a copy of the Prospective Adopter's Report with chronology, family support map and genogram;

- around two dozen inflated balloons for the exercise *Why adoption support is vital*.

Introductions/warm-up exercise

Choose one of the exercises listed on pp 24–26 to put the group at their ease and to get them to introduce themselves to each other.

SLIDE Learning outcomes

This session will help you to:

- understand what the journey to adoption will involve
- understand the assessment process and why it is necessary

Preparing to adopt

- understand more about how children and adopters are matched with each other
- understand why adopters may need support, both at the start and in the long term

Presentation

The agency

- Briefly describe your own agency, its ethos and its strengths.

- If you are a local authority agency, discuss the adoption map and scorecard in relation to your authority. If you are a voluntary adoption agency, discuss your statistics in relation to your assessment of adopters.

- You can explain any policies your agency has in place but be aware of statutory guidance, which sets out that 'Adoption agencies must not refuse to accept a registration of interest on the grounds of, for example, a prospective adopter's ethnicity, age, health, sexual orientation, religious beliefs or because they do not share the same ethnicity, culture or religious beliefs as the children waiting for an adoptive family.'

Information for trainers

The Government is keen to shorten the time taken for adoptions to go through and to remove barriers for people who want to adopt. In 2012, the Government produced an "adoption map" showing the numbers of children needing adoption in different areas of the country. It also introduced "adoption scorecards", ranking local councils according to how long, on average, children in their area wait to be adopted.

At the time of writing, on average, children in England wait 20 months to be adopted from the time they are taken into care. The new target is to place children with a family within 14 months (and, within this time, matching the child to a family within seven months of the court order being made).

However, "adoption scorecards" need to be treated with a degree of caution. Some areas have a greater proportion of children, e.g. sibling groups and older children, who take longer to be placed and of course the quality of placements is as important as the speed of placements.

Presentation

Your journey to adoption

- Explain the two-stage preparation process, with reference to the flowchart in the Workbook.

The adoption process

- Emphasise the diverse range of applicants and families who will be able to successfully adopt.

- Stress that there is no such thing as the "perfect family".

- Make the point that no one has the *right* to adopt. Adoption is principally about meeting the needs of children but prospective adopters looking to build their family through adoption should also have their needs considered.

Note to trainers

For more information about the two-stage adoption process, timescales and so on, see *Introduction*.

If this information has been covered in earlier meetings, e.g. information evenings, you will be able to go through this fairly quickly.

Exercise

What is adoption like for a child?

This exercise symbolises the way the child may have to give up various aspects of her identity when joining an adoptive family.

Participants draw and cut out a paper doll that represents themselves. Ask them to write on the doll's head and on both arms and legs five things that they feel are important parts of their identity: e.g. 'I am Scottish', 'I am a vegetarian', 'I am a dentist', 'I am artistic', 'I am a sister', etc. Then ask them to cut off one of the doll's limbs or its head and do a swap with the person next to them, using sticky tape to fasten this other limb/head into place instead. Repeat this cutting and swapping twice more. Participants will end up with a paper doll with mismatched and ill-fitting limbs or an arm in place of a leg, etc.

Encourage participants to reflect on the way that losing important parts of themselves feels a little uncomfortable. Help them to consider what adoption can mean for a child – there are losses as well as gains. Adopted children are gaining many things through adoption (loving parent(s), a nice home, etc.), but these things won't feel as though they "fit", at least at first. This is just one reason why adoptive parenting is different from other parenting, and why prospective adopters have to go through the processes of preparation and assessment.

Show DVD clip

Show the clip from the DVD in which Jade and Jordan, both adopted young people, talk about becoming adopted and what adoption means for them.

Preparing to adopt

Presentation

The assessment process

Here, you should refer to the home study and the Prospective Adopter's Report (PAR).

Explain what happens in the home study and reassure the group that it might not be as bad as some of them perhaps expect. Tell them that it is a chance for each of them to think about what would work for them and their family, what skills they have and what skills they may need to develop, and what support they are likely to have.

Ask the applicants why they think there are questions about their life experiences, and why they are asked to reflect on these.

SLIDE The role of the assessor

The social worker who assesses you will:

- carry out the "home study" – visit you at home and get to know you
- complete the Prospective Adopter's Report
- include a proposal to the panel about your suitability to adopt
- advise on the age range, likely needs and number of children you may be suitable to adopt

SLIDE The Prospective Adopter's Report looks at:

Family and environmental factors:

- family background and early experience
- adult life – work, health and other issues
- relationships and support networks
- the home, financial circumstances and lifestyle

SLIDE Becoming adopters

The assessment of parenting capacity considers your:

- motivation to adopt
- expectations of placement

The adoption process

- understanding of the needs of adopted children
- adoptive parenting capacity

SLIDE How will you be assessed?

- by asking you about yourself
- by asking others about you
- by self-assessment

Note to trainers

Explain that the process of assessment is done by:

- asking you about yourself, your background, your relationships and your motivation to adopt;
- face-to-face discussions to explore your personality, values, knowledge, skills and understanding of children's needs;
- assessing how well you could cope with the demands of adoptive parenting and what support systems you have;
- asking other people about you via personal references and discussion (Stage One and Stage Two);
- self-assessment;
- questionnaires, ecomaps, chronologies, etc., which you complete.

Using the slides that follow, explain how and why the recommendation must be evidence-based and not subjective or based on personal opinion. Explain that assessment must be underpinned by respect and empathy for the applicant, and openness and honesty in all exchanges between the worker and the applicant. Explain why it is important for applicants to be honest with their assessing social worker.

Tell the participants that assessment is subject to "quality control" by managers and supervisors; statutory guidance states that there may be a second opinion visit where clarification is needed or concerns have been raised, but not routinely. Put this into the context of your agency's procedure.

Explain the move towards "exchange" and "empowerment" models of assessment, which make for a more equal relationship between the assessor and the applicant.

Preparing to adopt

SLIDE The principles of assessment

Assessments are:

- evidence-based
- anti-discriminatory
- respectful
- open
- quality-controlled

SLIDE The exchange model of assessment

- You are the expert on yourself
- The social worker learns from you
- The social worker helps you identify your strengths and resources
- The social worker enables you to reach your goal

Presentation by approved adopter

You could invite a recently approved and/or matched adopter to talk about their experience of the assessment process. You could also refer participants to the Applicant's Workbook, in which there are contributions from adopters about how it was for them.

Presentation

How a child is identified and matched with you

- Briefly refer to the child's journey to adoption
- Briefly go through the family-finding and matching process
- Briefly describe what typically happens during introductions and how a child would move from the foster carer's home to the adopter's home

Note to trainers

The child's journey to adoption is covered more fully in the module *What is adoption?*. Family-finding and introductions are covered more fully in the module *Linking, matching and introductions*.

The adoption process

Q & A exercise

Ask participants to write down any questions they have about the assessment process and matching, anonymously, and put them in a box.

Then ask members of the group to draw out a question from the box, at random, and to read them aloud. You should answer each question in turn as fully as you can. If you don't know the answer to a question, tell the group that you will try to find out.

Note to trainers

This exercise allows group members to ask questions that they might otherwise feel awkward or embarrassed about asking, and you should stress that no question is considered silly or "off limits".

You may wish to provide them with identical slips of paper for this purpose so that no one can identify the writer of each question.

If anyone in the group has difficulty in writing, allow them to pair up with someone else to write their questions.

Presentation

Learning about you and your family

- Discuss the family support map and genogram and show the group what they look like – samples are provided in the Workbook.

- Encourage them to make a start on these themselves during Stage One; they will discuss and, if necessary, complete them with their social worker during Stage Two.

- Invite questions.

- Refer participants to pp 37–43 in their Workbook, reproduced from *Undertaking an Adoption Assessment* (Dibben, 2013), and which will help applicants to explore what adoption will mean for them.

Information for trainers

Different agencies may have different policies on whether they want adopters to make a start on these materials; participants' level of ability and confidence to complete them will also vary. If participants start on the chronology, family support map and genogram in Stage One, these can be used as assessment tools in Stage Two for the worker to further explore family relationships, dynamics and history.

Preparing to adopt

Exercise

Why adoption support is vital

Provide around two dozen inflated balloons. Ask for two volunteers, who should join you at the front of the room. Read out (or ask the participants to suggest) a list of tasks for all parents. Each time you name a different task, hand the volunteers a balloon each. These tasks could include, for instance:

- day-to-day care of the child;
- settling the child into school and supporting him or her with school work and activities;
- taking the child to football, parties and so on;
- taking the child to medical appointments;
- teaching the child to cross the road;
- teaching the child about safety online.

Now ask participants to suggest additional tasks required by adoptive parents. Load up one of the participants with these extra balloons too. For example, the tasks could include:

- explaining adoption to the child when he or she is a toddler;
- talking about adoption when the child is 10;
- talking to a teenager who is curious about her birth family;
- maintaining contact with the child's birth mother;
- maintaining contact with siblings in another family;
- negotiating changes in contact arrangements;
- taking the child to therapy because of past abuse;
- keeping her life story book alive and updating it.

At some point during this list, the participant will be unable to hold all the balloons and will start to drop some. Point out that the task of adoption is also too much for one person to cope with alone.

Ask the group to suggest other people who might be able to help – such as friends, family, another adopter, the family doctor, social worker or adoption agency. As each possible source of help is suggested, a group member comes to the front to represent that person and is given one of the balloons to hold.

Explain to participants that, if and when they become adoptive parents, they will have a lot of things to juggle and it is only natural that they will need help at times. Members of the

The adoption process

group will be able to support each other after the course is over, but there will be many other people or agencies who can also help.

- Explain that adoption is a lifelong task – having a child placed with you is just the beginning.
- Explain that even the most "capable" adopters are likely to need support at one stage or another – this is normal and doesn't mean you are not up to the task.

Presentation

Adoption support

First, provide each participant with a copy of the Adoption Passport that you have printed from the First4Adoption website (www.first4adoption.org.uk).

SLIDE The Adoption Passport (1)

- Priority in schools admission
- Free early education from age two
- Assessment of your child's needs
- Pupil Premium

SLIDE The Adoption Passport (2)

Adopters may be entitled to:

- Adoption leave and pay
- Counselling
- Therapeutic help for child
- Financial support, e.g. for special care needs
- Help with contact issues
- Meetings and events for adoptive families
- Training for adopters
- Short breaks for adopted children

Preparing to adopt

SLIDE Adoption support

- Every local authority has an "adoption support services adviser" (ASSA)
- Adopters are entitled to an assessment of their *need* for support
- What support they actually get will depend on circumstances
- LA or "personal budget"
- Assessment: whose responsibility?

Note to trainers

The Government's new "Adoption Passport" sets out the support that adopters in England may be entitled to.

- Children adopted from care have priority access to schools, which means that the child should be able to attend the school of his/her parents' choice.

- From September 2014, adopted children are entitled to free early education from the age of two.

- Adopters may be entitled to adoption leave and pay.

- Additional entitlements are being made available from April 2015, e.g. time off for introductions.

- Adopters may get priority for council housing.

- Adopters have the right to have their needs for support assessed – however, there is currently no duty on the local authority to *provide* this support to any individual adopter. Provision of services will depend on the adopters' circumstances.

- Future changes in the law mean that those receiving adoption support will be able to decide how it is provided, either by local authorities or through a "personal budget" to purchase services from a voluntary adoption agency or adoption support agency. The Government has announced that an Adoption Support Fund is being established in England from 2015.

- The local authority that places the child is responsible for assessing and (where appropriate) providing adoption support services for three years after the adoption order is made. After three years, this becomes the responsibility of the local authority where the adopters live (if this is different from the placing authority). The exception is that financial support and any contact arrangements agreed by the placing authority before the adoption order is made remain the responsibility of the placing authority.

The Pupil Premium was initially introduced for children adopted after 30 December 2005, but in May 2014, the Government issued guidance extending this to *all* adopted children.

The adoption process

More in-depth information about adoption support and therapies for adopted children will be provided in the Stage Two module, *Life as an adoptive family – learning to live together*.

SLIDE Other sources of support

- Your agency's own post-adoption support service
- BAAF
- Adoption UK
- First4Adoption
- Other adopters (and online communities for adopters)
- Other adopter support groups, e.g. New Family Social (UK network for lesbian, gay, bisexual and transgender adoptive and foster families)
- Adoption support agencies

Presentation

Support from this agency

Explain briefly what your agency can provide in the way of adoption support, e.g. financial support, family days, therapeutic help and so on.

Show DVD clip: The voice of the child

Show the clip that features children talking about waiting to be adopted/meeting adoptive parents.

To conclude

Summarise the messages you would like adopters to take away from this session. It might go something like this:

In the past, the adoption process has been criticised for taking too long and assessment has been deemed to be intrusive and subjective. The adoption process, preparation and assessment have undergone some changes recently. Assessment of prospective adopters is still thorough and it is still sometimes challenging for them. But there are good reasons for that. And we hope that now you understand these reasons better. We hope you also understand that you may need to access support at any stage of your child's childhood and adolescence – not just at the outset.

Preparing to adopt

You may wish to end the session with the closing exercise on page 26 or another exercise of your choice.

Suggested reading for trainers

Adoption passport on First4Adoption website (www.first4adoption.org.uk)

Department for Education (2013) *Statutory Guidance on Adoption:* Chapter 3, Preparing Assessing and Approving Prospective Adopters; Chapter 9, Adoption Support Services

Dibben E (2013) *Undertaking an Adoption Assessment*, London: BAAF

MODULE 4

Children's development and attachment

Timing

This module will take approximately two-and-a-half hours. With a larger group it is likely to take longer.

Setting the scene

- Introduce yourself and explain your role in the agency.

- Remind the group where this module fits into your agency's schedule of training for prospective adopters. If this module marks the start of Stage Two, explain to the group that this stage of preparation looks in more depth at the tasks facing them as prospective adopters and aims to equip them with the knowledge, understanding and skills they will need.

- Refer to housekeeping issues (e.g. fire escapes, toilets, timing of breaks and the time the session will end).

- Explain and outline the ground rules listed in the *Introduction* on page 17.

  For this module you will need:

- a large ball of string, scissors and some sticky tape;

- sheets of A4 paper and felt pens for the exercise *The bricks in the wall*.

Introductions/warm-up exercise

Choose one of the exercises listed on pp 24–26 to put the group at their ease and to get them to introduce themselves to each other.

SLIDE Learning outcomes

The aim of this session is to help you understand more about:

- children's developmental needs
- the impact of adversity in early life
- the importance of attachment for babies and children
- how bonds of attachment are formed
- what can go wrong in attachment
- children's identity needs

77

Preparing to adopt

Presentation

Children's development

Outline to the group several examples of a child's behaviour that does not fit the usual sequential pattern. For instance:

- a child who can put together three-word sentences but cannot sit up;
- a child who can hop, but who is not toilet-trained during the day;
- a child who can count objects up to five, but cannot put on her jumper.

Ask them for their reaction. Ask them if this behaviour seems "normal". If not, what is not "normal" about it?

Introduce the idea of child development and the way in which it happens sequentially, with abilities developing in the same order, i.e. *a* then *b* then *c*. Non-sequential behaviour is a consequence of genetic impairment in one or more areas, physical/emotional trauma at some point (possibly pre-birth) or adverse environmental factors.

Now, give out the *Children's Development Quiz* handout and ask the group to consider "normal" child development by doing the quiz (working in small groups). Then go through the answers on the *Children's Development Quiz Answers* handout with them.

At the end of the exercise, suggest that as homework they read the section on child development, including the charts, in their Workbook.

HANDOUT

Quiz: Children's development

1. At approximately what age would you expect a baby to have doubled his birth weight?
2. At approximately what age would you expect a baby to roll over from her front to her back?
3. At approximately what age would you expect a baby to be able to sit unsupported for up to 10 minutes?
4. At approximately what age would you expect a child to be able to climb stairs without help (using alternating feet on consecutive stairs)?
5. At approximately what age would you expect a child to be able to hop on one foot?
6. At approximately what age would you expect a child to begin to be able to understand about taking turns?
7. At approximately what age would you expect a child to put together two or more words?

Children's development and attachment

8. At approximately what age would you expect a child to be able to understand riddles?
9. At what age would you expect a child to be "clean and dry" during the day?
10. At what age would you expect a child to be able to use a knife and fork?

HANDOUT

Children's development: answers to quiz

1. six months
2. five months
3. eight months
4. four years
5. four years
6. three to four years
7. from 10 months onwards
8. eight years
9. two-and-a-half years
10. seven years (to use a knife properly)

Show DVD clip

Show the clip from the DVD which illustrates reciprocity between parent and baby – *Serve and Return interaction shapes brain architecture*. This is produced by the Center on the Developing Child at Harvard University, http://developingchild.harvard.edu.

Presentation

Reciprocity

The developing relationship between a healthy baby and a sensitive and responsive caregiver is reciprocal. They learn to respond to each other's behaviour and mood. The baby learns that the caregiver is reliably there for her and can understand and provide for her needs.

Stress the importance of both parent and baby providing cues to each other. The parent attends to the baby with eye contact, smiles, talking and singing; the baby responds by gurgling and cooing and moving her arms and legs about.

Preparing to adopt

What happens to the child during the first weeks, months and years of her life – in particular, her interactions with her caregivers – shapes the way her brain develops and has a profound effect on every aspect of her development. If all goes well, the baby develops a sense of basic trust and security.

Remind participants that a baby who has experienced inappropriate care or disrupted attachments may develop attachment difficulties. This can significantly affect her behaviour in later childhood, her emotional development and her relationships. She may become the kind of child who does not "reward" carers with the affection they hope for.

Notes for trainers

Definitions

Attachment: The feeling/need child has for a particular adult or small group of adults.

Bonding: The process by which an adult grows to love a child.

Attachment behaviour: The things that a child does to get an adult to respond and stay close, e.g. crying, smiling, gurgling, following.

The function of attachment behaviour is protection plus physical and emotional survival. Unlike other primate infants, human babies cannot physically cling to or follow their parent so must develop an alternative way of keeping the parent close. Attachment is also key in helping a baby to begin to learn how to regulate emotion.

The following presentation looks at attachment and attachment difficulties in more detail.

Presentation

Attachment

With the help of the following slides, explain how attachment develops, the importance of attachment, types of attachment and what happens when bonds are disrupted.

Ask participants to read the section on attachment in their Workbook (pp 48–56) after the session.

SLIDE How attachment develops

- Claiming
- Attunement
- Affective attunement

Children's development and attachment

- Impulse regulation
- Shame regulation
- Rage management
- Pre-cognitive patterning

Information for trainers

The following information is drawn from *Building Identity: A training programme* (Cairns and Fursland, 2008).

These are the seven stages by which babies become attached to their carers. Disruption or distortion of any of these stages is likely to have a far-reaching impact on the way the child functions and how she feels about herself.

Claiming

This is the first stage in attachment, in which key attachment figures recognise the newborn baby as their own and take responsibility for caring for her.

Attunement

Attunement is the mutual and reciprocal relationship that develops as a carer and baby learn more about each other's responses, and their bodies and brains, feelings and thoughts begin to work in tune with each other. The baby feels stress when she is hot, cold, uncomfortable or frightened. She cries. This is a sound that makes the carer feel stressed and uncomfortable, so the carer responds by meeting the baby's need and soothing her. As the carer feeds or soothes the baby, the carer's breathing slows down and his or her muscles relax and the baby follows suit. Because of the attention of the carer, the baby learns that stress is followed by soothing and relaxing. She learns to trust that her needs will be met. This is the foundation of being able to trust other people.

The baby will smile, coo and gurgle at the carer and this gives the carer pleasure so he or she responds to the baby; the carer's smiles, voice and attention are rewarding, so the baby does it some more.

Affective attunement

This develops when the baby tunes in to the carer's feelings and emotions. The baby will feel stressed when the carer is stressed and she will become distressed if she sees the carer distressed. This is the start of being able to identify with other people.

Preparing to adopt

Impulse regulation and shame regulation

We all have to learn to control our impulses if we are to be able to live in harmony with other people and obey society's rules. But young children need to be able to do this before they are able to think logically about rules or to understand why running into the road or pushing another child over is a bad idea.

Young children learn to control impulses through the feeling of shame. This is how it works: when a toddler does something that could be dangerous to herself or someone else, an attuned carer reacts immediately to stop her from doing it. The carer's reaction temporarily breaks the attunement between the child and carer. The child, often visibly shocked by this sudden change in the relationship, experiences shame and stops what she is doing.

For the securely attached toddler, attunement is quickly re-established. When she controls her impulses, she is quickly rewarded by the reinstatement of the usual warmth and positive attention from the carer.

Of course, this process depends on attunement: an attuned carer will notice what the child is doing and react appropriately; the attuned child responds to this reaction by feeling shame. If attunement is lacking in the first place, neither of these things may happen.

Some experts believe that this process of impulse control through shame starts at around nine months and continues for around nine months. By 18 months, the brain is developed enough for the child to be able to feel and think about social behaviour, social discipline and self-discipline.

Rage management

As the child develops, she gains a sense of herself as being separate from others. She realises that the world beyond herself can be the source of unpleasant feelings such as frustration, shame and fear. This can make her want to lash out and destroy whatever is producing the unpleasant feelings.

Young children can experience a powerful sense of rage in relation to something that seems small to us. Rage comes from the limbic part of the brain called the amygdala, which is involved in the production of basic survival instincts. In adults, the limbic brain is usually kept "under control" by the activity of the cortex, which is the "thinking" brain. We consider the situation and decide on the response we want to make. But in young children, the cortex is still developing. Young children do not have the connections between the cortex and the limbic system that would allow them to transmit inhibitory signals and restrain the activity of the amygdala.

Most children are helped to manage and later to inhibit their own rage as a result of interaction with secure attachment figures. This helps to pattern the pathways in the brain to ensure that anger can be inhibited by the cortex.

This rage, this impulse to destroy, is the most powerful of the impulses that need to be regulated. Children who are unable to manage stress or control their impulses will not be

Children's development and attachment

able to manage their rage either. To other people they may come across as volatile, unpredictable, threatening or even violent.

Differentiation

In the first year of life, the baby has no sense of herself as having a separate identity from her caregivers. Through attachment, babies learn both to identify with others and to differentiate from them. A baby develops a sense of herself as being similar to others in some ways but also different and unique. This is her sense of identity.

Pre-cognitive patterning

In the first year, the baby cannot yet process her feelings or "think", but something called pre-cognitive patterning does take place. Repeated cycles build certain patterns in the baby's brain – perhaps a sense of safety, a repeated sense of stress relieved by soothing and relaxation, the difference between night and day, how best to gain "control" of caregivers so that they will respond to her needs, and so on. These patterns will affect how the child can think later on in the developmental process.

During years 2 to 6, the cortex, or "thinking" brain, is developing. This allows abstract thought, and the functioning of this part of the brain will determine many of the individual attributes that make up the growing personality: creativity, abstract reasoning, humour, verbal competence, artistic flair and so on.

SLIDE Why is attachment important?

- A strong attachment is vital for a child's healthy development in many different spheres
- Unmet attachment needs can affect the way the child thinks, feels and behaves for years to come
- If early attachments have been dysfunctional, the child may have distorted perceptions of adult–child relationships

Information for trainers

The positive effects of attachment

A strong attachment can enable a child to do the following:

- *Attain his/her full intellectual potential*
- *Sort out what he/she perceives*
- *Think logically*

Preparing to adopt

- *Develop social emotions*
- *Develop a conscience*
- *Trust others*
- *Become self-reliant*
- *Cope better with stress and frustration*
- *Reduce feelings of jealousy*
- *Overcome common fears and worries*
- *Increase feelings of self-worth*

(Fahlberg, 1994, p 14)

How does attachment develop?

- Depends on quality of emotional relationship
- Depends on successful care-providing interaction between parent and child

SLIDE The arousal–relaxation cycle

(Reproduced from *A Child's Journey through Placement* by Vera Fahlberg, 1994)

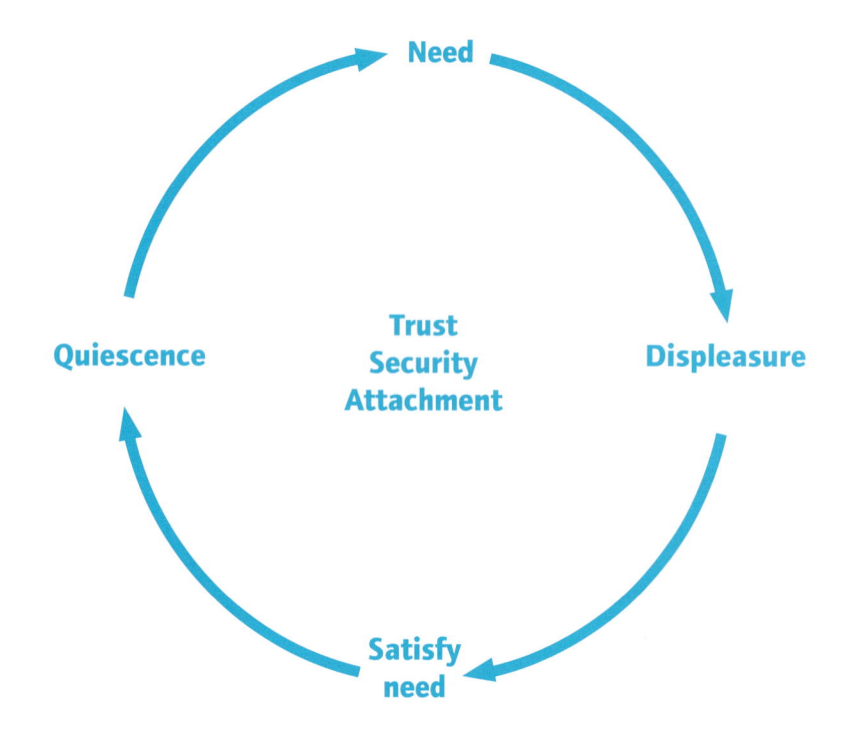

```
              Need
               ↓
Quiescence   Trust        Displeasure
             Security
             Attachment
               ↑
            Satisfy
             need
```

Children's development and attachment

SLIDE Stages of attachment

- Birth – child can tell people apart
- Up to six months – may show preference for main carer
- 7–10 months – develops specific attachments
- 10–18 months – child upset when separated from attachment figures
- 18 months–2 years – child can explore from safe and secure base (trusted adult)
- 3 years – attachments strong, dependence decreases
- 4.5–5 years – child can cope with longer separations but still needs to return to base if distressed or threatened.

Show DVD clip

Show the clip which illustrates the arousal–relaxation cycle.

Information for trainers

Stages of attachment

Children reach these stages at slightly different times, just as they reach physical milestones at different times.

- Children can differentiate one person from another from birth.
- Up to six months, the child may show preference for one person but will accept care from different people.
- At about seven to 10 months, the child develops a specific attachment to one or more people.
- At 10–18 months, attachment is intensified. Distress is alleviated only by object of attachment – child responds to small group of trusted, familiar adults.
- At 18 months–2 years, the attached child can explore the world around, providing that physical access to an attachment figure is maintained. Danger/distress causes child to need to return quickly to base (i.e. trusted adult).
- At 3+ years, attachments are strong/secure (experience has taught that attachment figure continues to exist when out of sight but will come back). Dependence decreases. Child can cope with short separations (hours).
- At 4–5 years, the child can cope with longer separations but distress/danger still triggers the need to return to base.
- The securely attached child develops trust in self/others/world.

Preparing to adopt

- Even where the child has secure attachment, repeated or prolonged separation from attachment figures causes distress and anxiety and halts development.

SLIDE Patterns of attachment

Patterns of attachment are strategies that a child has developed in order to keep the carer close and in order to feel as safe as possible.

- Secure attachment
- Insecure attachment:
  - Anxious/resistant/ambivalent
  - Anxious/compliant
- Anxious/avoidant/dismissive attachment
- Disorganised attachment

Information for trainers

Children who have not been able to build an attachment properly (because their caregiver has not provided a secure base) will have difficulties with attachment later on. The nature of their attachment patterns will vary, depending on the interaction they have or had with the caregiver, and with their age.

Patterns of attachment

Secure attachment

Parent/attachment figure:

- is physically and emotionally available to child
- interprets child's needs accurately and responds appropriately

Child:

- sees parent as source of safety and security

Young child:

- shows distress at separation
- greets parent/attachment figure positively on reunion

Children's development and attachment

Child has:

- ability to form and sustain close, stable and intimate relationships
- self-confidence, self-esteem, competence, trust and empathy

Insecure attachment

- Anxious/resistant/ambivalent
- Anxious/compliant

Parent:

- is insensitive to child's needs
- responds inappropriately
- is inconsistent/unpredictable
- is not consistently available for child either physically or emotionally

Child:

- sees parent as not available or not responsive or both. Child either becomes highly dependent, eager to please and compliant, or ambivalent – continuously demanding parental attention, but resisting approaches from parent
- is aggressive and cannot maintain relationships with adults or peers

Young child:

- is fearful and agitated when parent leaves, and difficult to calm on reunion

Anxious/avoidant/dismissive attachment

Parent is:

- indifferent to or rejecting of child's needs

Child:

- sees parent as likely to reject/rebuff and therefore becomes emotionally self-sufficient
- has difficulty in forming and sustaining relationships
- avoids emotional closeness
- expects to be rejected
- is compulsively self-reliant

Preparing to adopt

Young child:

- appears unperturbed when parent leaves
- ignores or avoids parent on return

Disorganised attachment

Parent is:

- ineffectual, helpless and/or hostile
- frightened and frightening (e.g. parent is mentally ill, abusive, involved in domestic violence)
- The parent who should provide protection for the child does not, and can actually be the source of danger.

Child:

- has unmanageable anxiety/confusion
- "freezes" physically and/or emotionally
- does not get involved in relationships, but is not emotionally self-sufficient

Young child:

- behaviour is confused and disorganised

Presentation

A child's damaged attachments: implications for adopters

SLIDE Damaged attachments: implications for adopters

- Damaged attachments can affect a child's capacity to form new attachments
- Child's behaviours can be puzzling and upsetting for adopters
- It can feel as though the child is rejecting them
- Child's behaviour in foster family may not predict how they will be with adopters
- When there's a possible match, discuss child's attachment history and needs

Children's development and attachment

Information for trainers

A lack of attachment, dysfunctional attachment and broken attachments can all affect the child's capacity to respond to care – these children may take a long time to feel or show affection for their adoptive parents.

Children may show a range of dysfunctional attachment behaviours (as described above) that can be difficult and wearing for their adopters. If a child appears to reject them and refuses to let them comfort her when she is hurt or upset, it can be hard for adopters to take. They want to love and nurture the child but they feel rebuffed. This is why it's crucial for prospective adopters to understand attachment and attachment difficulties. Later sessions will explain how adopters can help a child to build new attachments.

Even if a child seems to be doing well with foster carers, that doesn't necessarily mean everything will be fine when she moves to the adoptive family. Adopters have different expectations of being able to bond with the child, and the child may cope less well with the emotional demands of being in an adoptive family.

Assessment may be far from easy if records are incomplete and/or the child has experienced several changes of carer and/or social worker, and where the only real evidence available is within their current placement. It is dangerous for both workers and carers to place too much emphasis on perceived progress in short-term care. Expectations and emotions are very different when permanence and commitment to a new family become a reality.

(Beesley, 2010, p 56)

Explain that if and when applicants are matched with a child, they will have the opportunity to find out about the individual child's attachment history and to discuss the child's needs and the possible consequences. They should seek the information they need to make informed decisions (but bear in mind the points made below).

Assessing a child's attachment needs

Promoting attachment

Some (children) will manifest a range of dysfunctional attachment behaviours…It is dangerous to underestimate the demands of caring for such children…the experience of adult adoptees and care leavers reminds us that the interruption of primary connections has consequences which are potentially lifelong, and may result in a deep sense of personal loss and/or rejection. Warm loving parenting can diminish the pain but to pretend that it can be completely healed is not helpful, and is one of the central issues that alternative families need to consider…

Careful preparation is essential in terms of helping new families to understand the child's attachment history alongside other aspects of their development and early experience. But understanding is only one part of the equation. Other aspects are managing the powerful emotions that caring for the child can generate, managing the lack of or desperately slow-to-

Preparing to adopt

develop attachment of the child, and persevering with and managing difficult behaviours. A further important part of the equation is helping the child to feel part of an adoptive/foster family and all that this entails for the family both internally (individually and as a family unit) and externally (relating to wider family, community and services available to support the family). Families will need skilled help and ongoing support.

(Beesley, 2010, p 63)

SLIDE Attachment when a baby has a disability or medical condition

- Baby may be unresponsive
- Baby may be in hospital for a long time
- Multiple carers
- Baby's receptiveness to parent may be affected
- Parent's reaction to news of baby's condition
- Depression in mother

Information for trainers

- A baby with impairments, e.g. foetal alcohol effects, may be unresponsive and fail to interact positively with the caregiver.
- Spending a long time in hospital early on may disrupt a baby's attachment formation.
- Multiple carers (e.g. nurses, respite foster carers) may have had to step in before the child has had a chance to develop secure attachments with primary caregivers.
- Impairment may affect child's receptiveness to parent's attachment behaviour, especially if poorly attuned – e.g. where a baby with visual impairment makes limited eye contact and the adult does not offer compensatory contact through touching or stroking.
- Medication might affect the baby's behaviour or mood, which could affect her ability to reciprocate.
- Parent's reaction on being told or discovering the baby's impairment may lead to difficulties with bonding.
- Depression in the mother (which might result from giving birth to a baby with impairments) can affect the way she interacts with the baby and can result in attachment difficulties.

Children's development and attachment

Exercise

The effect of repeated separations on a child

Allocate to participants the roles of the child and significant people in her life:

- the child, Lexy;
- birth mother, Jade;
- brother, Mark;
- sister, Jodie;
- Jade's parents, Jim and Moira;
- Jade's boyfriend, Jez;
- the social worker;
- foster carers, Hannah and John;
- foster carers, Sheila and Barry;
- adoptive mother, Sarah.

The participant who is representing the child, Lexy, stands in middle of a circle made up of the other "characters" in the fictional account below. As you read out the story, at relevant points give Lexy a piece of string to hold – the other end of the string should be given to and held by the person indicated in the story. With each separation, cut the relevant piece of string. At certain points in the story you will need to re-connect some pieces with sticky tape.

At the end of the story Lexy will be left standing in the middle, holding a lot of pieces of broken string. Now just two pieces of string connect her to other people: one to her adoptive mother and the other to her sister.

Discuss this exercise with the group.

- Ask the person who took the part of Lexy how it feels to have so many broken pieces of string.
- Ask the person who took the part of the adoptive mother, Sarah, how she would feel about helping Lexy to maintain any of these relationships in some form, e.g. with her birth mother, Jade, and with her brother, Mark, who may be adopted into another family.
- Introduce the idea of contact, which is explored more fully in Module 8, *Telling, contact and social networking*.

Lexy's story

Lexy was born to 22-year-old Jade who had two older children, three-year-old Mark and two-year-old Jodie. (*Tie three pieces of string to connect Lexy with Jade, Mark and Jodie.*)

Preparing to adopt

Jade was separated from Andy, the father of Mark and Jodie. He had gone abroad and no one knew where he was. At the time she conceived Lexy, Jade was living in a squat, drinking and smoking a lot of cannabis and had multiple sexual partners so was not sure who Lexy's father was. Jade moved in with her parents during her pregnancy and she left most of the child care to her parents, Jim and Moira, who tried to support her and the children as well as they could. When Lexy was born, Jade had little interest in her. (*Give Lexy two more pieces of string and give the other ends to Jim and Moira.*)

But when Lexy was seven months old, Jade met a new boyfriend, Jez, and after a couple of months she moved in with him and took the children with her. (*Cut the strings held by Moira and Jim. Give Lexy a string to connect her with Jez.*)

However, it soon became clear that Jez was a violent man and after six months Jade and the children moved into a women's refuge. (*Cut the string to Jez.*) They were there for three months. At first Moira and Jim said they couldn't cope with having Jade and the children back, because of their own ill-health. But they relented and Jade and the children moved back, with Moira and Jim again providing much of the childcare. (*Using sticky tape, re-connect two of Lexy's strings with the ends held by Moira and Jim.*)

When Lexy was two years old, Jim died suddenly. (*Cut the string held by Jim.*) Moira was grief-stricken and became depressed and unable to look after the children. In addition, by this time her arthritis had got worse and she was unable to do the physical caring they needed. Jade was drinking heavily. She agreed that the children should be taken into care. (*Cut the strings held by Jade and Moira.*)

The three children were fostered by short-term foster carers Hannah and John. (*Give new strings to connect Lexy to Hannah and John.*)

Three months later, Jade said she wanted the children back. She was asked to attend an assessment unit with the children for six weeks. (*Cut the strings to Hannah and John; re-connect the string to Jade.*) But in spite of Jade being offered support for her alcohol abuse, she was unable to stop drinking and provide the care the children needed. The local authority applied for a care order.

The children went to another set of foster carers, Sheila and Barry. (*Cut the string to Jade; give two more strings to Lexy with the other ends to be held by Sheila and Barry.*) By now Mark was showing disturbed behaviour. Sheila and Barry found it extremely demanding to look after him. The children's social worker assessed their needs and it was decided that they needed to be adopted, but that Mark should be adopted separately from his sisters as he needed one-to-one care as the only child in an adoptive family.

When Lexy was three and Jodie was five, they were placed with Sarah for adoption. (*Cut the strings to Sheila, Barry and Mark. Give Lexy a string to connect her to Sarah.*)

Note to trainers

The story of Lexy also features in an earlier module, where it is used in a different way.

Children's development and attachment

Presentation

Loss and grief

SLIDE The stages of grief

In 1969, Elizabeth Kubler-Ross devised the Grief Cycle model in which she identified the stages of grief:

1 Shock
2 Denial
3 Anger
4 Bargaining
5 Sadness and despair
6 Resolution

SLIDE Separation and loss

- Separations from attachment figures (even inadequate or abusive parents) represent losses for a child
- Separation from a mother at birth is still a loss
- Children need to go through the different stages of grief, just as adults do
- They may express it by their behaviour rather than verbally
- Children who are unable to grieve may become "stuck"
- Certain events or times of year may remind the child of their loss
- Adopters need to be aware of the child's grief and be sensitive to changes of mood and behaviour

SLIDE Loss through adoption

It differs from other types of loss in several ways:

- The loss may be felt as a rejection
- There is no end to the loss and the rejection
- The cause is often unclear (to the child)

Preparing to adopt

- Nothing is finite and information can change overnight
- It is often not socially acceptable to be angry or sad about adoption
- Society sees adoption as positive – and the notion of "gratitude" can result in adopted children not daring to grieve openly at home

(Wolfs, 2010)

SLIDE Dealing with grief

- For adopted children, the process of grieving is complicated and difficult
- They will vary in how they express their feelings and how intensely they feel
- They will need support from adopters to deal with it
- They will need help in recognising and accepting the pain
- Grieving results from being given up/taken away from birth family, not the adoption itself
- The child will continue to experience the loss at different developmental moments, e.g. puberty

(Wolfs, 2010)

Information for trainers

Separation and loss are major themes in the lives of children adopted and in foster care, whether it is the infant separated from a mother at birth or the older child who has experienced separation from birth parents and siblings plus a number of moves within the care system. Children require time to grieve and to pass through the different stages of grief just like any adult who has experienced a bereavement. Children's grieving process can take years, and the difficulty for some children is not having the space to grieve, their energies often being focused on survival. Adults often expect children to be able to adjust to major changes in their lives without due recognition of the impact. Children who are unable to grieve may become "stuck" developmentally, unable to move beyond the stage of anger, denial or despair. Much of their emotional energy is taken up with the pain associated with their loss and there is little left over for growth or movement. Children may close down emotionally and, because their development is "stuck", they may function below their chronological age emotionally, cognitively and behaviourally. As we know, children are more likely to communicate their feelings through behaviour. Grief may be expressed through acting out, anger and aggression, but it can also manifest itself through withdrawal and depression.

Applicants need to understand the significance of loss in children's lives and be sensitive to their moods and behaviour…Sensitivity to major events such as birthdays and Christmas or

Children's development and attachment

other festive occasions, the changing of the seasons, the start of a school term, anything that serves as a poignant reminder to the child of their loss, will help later on when, as new parents, they see a sudden, seemingly unexpected, change of mood or behaviour in their child. Understanding the need for appropriate regression, and thinking about how they will teach or model a range of feelings, will be important.

(Beesley, 2010, pp 168–169)

The US psychologist David Brodzinsky has identified a stage of "adapted" grieving when the child, even if adopted as an infant, comes to understand cognitively that their adoption may have involved loss or rejection. This is sometimes manifested as difficult and puzzling behaviour coming "out of the blue" and is often associated with children in the latency years, aged eight to 11. Sometimes there are also fears about the permanency of their adoptive family as they have already "lost" one family.

Exercise

The bricks in the wall

This exercise presents a symbolic representation of a childhood in which a child has not been given the care necessary for healthy development.

Ask participants to divide into groups. Ask each group to consider one of the following age ranges:

- 0–6 months
- 6 months–2 years
- 2–5 years
- 5–9 years
- 9–12 years
- 12–16 years

Provide them with a number of pieces of A4-sized paper. Ask them to discuss within the group and come up with 10 things that they think a child (in their age group) needs for healthy development and attachments. For example, these things should relate to the kind of care and the experiences that children need at different ages – eye contact, cuddles, milk, food, boundaries, security, trust, friends and so on. When they have decided on the 10 things, ask them to write these on the pieces of paper (one per sheet). The different groups may come up with some of the same words – that is fine.

Now ask the participants to build a "wall" with their "bricks" (represented by the sheets of paper) on the floor in the middle of the room, where everyone can see.

Starting with the group that considered babies up to six months, ask one member of the

Preparing to adopt

group to start building a wall by laying their "bricks" down. As this person places the "bricks", he or she should read out the word on each one.

Now do the same with the second group, which was considering children from six months to two years. Ask someone from the second group to build another row of "bricks" above the first row of the existing wall – each time they place a "brick" they should read out what is written on it.

Do the same with the other groups. The wall should now be looking fairly robust.

Draw a parallel with a child who has been given everything she needs in terms of care and nurturing and who is developing in a healthy way.

Now ask participants to consider the experiences of some of the children they have heard about during the course – children like Lexy, in the previous exercise, and children in the case studies and so on. Ask the group what these children might have missed out on in terms of the nurturing experiences they should have had (from those things mentioned on the bricks).

As people suggest various nurturing experiences that children may have lacked, take out the relevant "brick" from the "wall" and remove it. In some cases, if the care or the experience has been inconsistent or erratic rather than completely absent (e.g. "milk" or "food"), you could simply dislodge the brick rather than remove it altogether. You may be able to make links as you remove or dislodge the bricks – e.g. if one brick is labelled "stimulation" and another is labelled "learning", explain that a child who has lacked "stimulation" at the age of two may have difficulties with "learning" later on.

As more of the bricks are removed from the structure or are dislodged, to represent the nurturing experiences children have missed out on, the wall starts to look more and more unstable. If it were a real wall, it would look to be in danger of collapsing.

Draw a parallel with children who have not had the love and care they should have had, who have not been able to develop strong attachments or who have not been given the attention and stimulation they need. These children will be fragile emotionally, socially and in other ways. It is the task of adopters to try to "rebuild" walls for these children.

Note for trainers

It will enhance this exercise if you can have an adopter or adopters leading it. Some agencies have an adopter, or even two, who are also trainers or who support the trainers. The adopter(s) can play an active part in this exercise by talking through their real experience of their own children. As the adopter(s) talks about their child's experiences at each stage they can rip up a piece of paper representing "food", "stimulation", "education", etc. If the adopters' children are now older you can include the older stages and the adopter can carry on ripping pieces out of the higher levels of bricks, showing how the neglect and other early experiences are still affecting the child now. This is very real and very effective. What is left is a shaky-looking but still functioning wall. After a break or another exercise the group can return to the dilapidated wall and the adopter(s) talk about "making it better", telling the group about all the things they have been able to put in place for their

Children's development and attachment

children to help them to "shore up" and repair the wall.

If you don't have any adopters who can help in this way, you could refer to case studies instead.

Exercise

Who am I?

Ask participants to individually jot down five words or phrases that would complete a sentence beginning 'I am...' if they were talking to someone about themselves. These should be words or phrases that they feel have some importance to them.

Ask them to discuss, in small groups:

- Are there any things on this list that you could change fairly easily?
- Are there things that would be very difficult for you to change?
- Are there things that would be impossible for you to change?

Introduce the idea that, as human beings, we form a sense of who we are in two ways: similarity to others and difference from others.

(This exercise is from Cairns and Fursland, 2008, p 9.)

SLIDE Similarities and differences

Similarity – we identify ourselves as similar to others

Difference – we identify ourselves as different from others

Ask participants to look at their lists again with "similarity" and "difference" in mind. They will realise that some of their words and phrases may indicate ways in which they identify with a group: 'I am Jewish', 'I am a Manchester United supporter', 'I am a member of the Labour Party', while others may be more to do with differentiation – 'I am a good cook', 'I am a person with a disability', 'I am someone who survived a bad car crash'.

Information for trainers

Both similarity (identification) with others and differentiation from others are important processes for humans and human societies.

But if identification with a group is overvalued in society it can lead to problems, e.g. football violence, gang membership, discrimination (and worse) against minority groups such as different ethnic groups, dissenting political or religious groups or lesbians and gay men.

Preparing to adopt

Problems can also occur when the emphasis on individualism is so great that there is little sense of community and people feel they don't "belong" anywhere.

There are parallels with life in families here – how much are the individual members of a family allowed to be "different"? How much do they feel they "belong" to the family (in a positive way)?

SLIDE A child's sense of identity

Children who have experienced neglect and abuse may have been:

- made to feel worthless
- rejected or belittled
- scapegoated within the family
- made to feel they are just a commodity to be exploited
- given negative messages about their gender, ethnicity, culture or disability or other things that make them "different"

Information for trainers

Children who have not been loved and cherished may have formed a negative sense of their own identity – they feel unlovable and they may think they are to blame for their losses and bad things that happen.

Exercise

Children and identity distortion

Ask participants to look at the following slide and to suggest examples for each of these points.

SLIDE Impairments and distortions in the process of identification

These may occur if children:

- Identify with people who harm them
- Receive negative messages about people with whom they identify

Children's development and attachment

- Receive negative messages about their gender, ethnicity, culture, disability and other things that make them different
- Are forced to identify with others against their will
- Are prevented from identifying with others
- Are unable to identify with others

Information for trainers

Here are some examples. The group will probably come up with others of their own.

- A child might identify with an older sibling who abused them.
- A child might identify with a birth family where there is violence or criminality.
- A child might have received negative messages from family members (birth or foster family) about birth relatives with whom she identifies.
- A girl may identify herself as being of less value than a boy.
- A child living in another country who is abducted from his family by an armed group and forced to become a child soldier is forced to identify with others against his will.
- A child of immigrant parents may have very different ideas and aspirations from those of her parents, but may be forced to comply with customs and cultural practices against her will.
- A child who is prevented from going to school or from mixing with other children is unable to identify with her peers.
- A black child who has been fostered in a white foster family may struggle to identify with them – or, lacking attachment figures of the same ethnicity as herself, she may identify with them and see herself as white.

SLIDE Tasks for adopters

The tasks for adopters include:

- accept the child as she is
- repair the damage done to a child's sense of identity
- help the child form a positive sense of who she is
- help the child feel that she "belongs"
- help the child to accept and be proud of the things that make her "different"

Preparing to adopt

Information for trainers

The aim of this exercise is to help participants to understand the importance of identification and differentiation and to start considering the effect of attachment and diversity issues on the child's sense of identity. There is more on identity and diversity in the module *Becoming a parent through adoption*.

The voice of the child: DVD clip

Show the video clip from the DVD of Heather and Ayesha talking about their lives in their adoptive families. Alternatively, you could read excerpts from *The Colours in Me* or some of the first-hand accounts from *Chosen: Living with adoption*, both edited by Perlita Harris.

To conclude

Summarise the messages you would like participants to take away from this session, along the lines set out below. Stress that this session has looked at what *should* happen in children's early experiences and at what can go wrong. Other Stage Two modules will explain how adopters can help children make new attachments and recover from their early adverse experiences.

The children who need adoption have had an unhappy start in life. They have not been given what they need for healthy development and, in many cases, have been damaged by this. Even those who formed good attachments as babies will have experienced loss and separation (sometimes multiple times) by the time they come to you. An important part of your job, if you become an adoptive parent, will be to put back some of the "bricks in the wall" and help the child to recover and form new attachments that will last. Many children do make considerable progress when they are placed with a loving adopter or adoptive family, even though it often takes some time.

You may wish to end with the closing exercise from page 26 or another closing exercise of your choice.

Suggested reading for trainers

Harris P (ed) (2008) *The Colours in Me*, London: BAAF

Harris P (ed) (2012) *Chosen: Living with adoption*, London: BAAF

Schofield G and Beek M (2006) *Attachment Handbook for Foster Care and Adoption*, London: BAAF

Schofield G and Beek M (2014) *The Secure Base Model: Promoting attachment and resilience using the Secure Base model*, London: BAAF

Verrier N (2009) *The Primal Wound*, London: BAAF

Verrier N (2010) *Coming Home to Self*, London: BAAF

References

Beesley P (2010) *Making Good Assessments* (2nd edn), London: BAAF

Cairns K and Fursland E (2008) *Building Identity: A training programme*, London: BAAF

Fahlberg V (1994) *A Child's Journey through Placement*, London: BAAF

Kübler-Ross E (1969) *On Death and Dying*, London: Routledge

Wolfs R (2008) *Adoption Conversations: What, when and how to tell*, London: BAAF

Wolfs R (2010) *More Adoption Conversations: What, when and how to tell*, London: BAAF

Preparing to adopt

MODULE 5

The needs of children affected by neglect and abuse

Timing

This module will take approximately three-and-a-half hours, not including a refreshment break.

Setting the scene

- Introduce yourself and explain your role in the agency.

- Remind participants where this module fits into your agency's programme of preparation training.

- Refer to housekeeping (e.g. location of fire escapes and toilets, timing of breaks, finish time).

- Remind them that the aim of Stage Two is to ensure they are prepared for what will lie ahead of them as an adoptive family and that they will be able to cope with the challenges. Some of the children whom members of the group may go on to adopt will have experienced neglect and abuse, and that is the focus of this session.

- Tell the group that the things spoken about in this session might be disturbing and distressing for some people and could even bring back unhappy memories of some people's own childhoods. Say that, if anyone needs to take a short break, they should feel free to go out for a few minutes and if anyone needs to talk about anything, they are welcome to come and see you at any time. (It is a good idea to ensure that you have enough trainers available in case one is needed to go out and spend time with a participant who is upset. Have a plan for how you will manage such a situation.)

- Remind participants of the ground rules (p 17) and invite them to add any other rules to the list.

What you will need

For this session you will need copies of the handout *Tina's story* and a selection of toys, pencils and crayons and paper.

Introductions/warm-up exercise

Choose an exercise from those listed on pp 24–26, or one of your own favourite exercises.

The needs of children

SLIDE Learning outcomes

The aim of this module is to help you understand the following:

- What do "neglect" and "abuse" actually mean?
- How does childhood trauma affect attachment and brain development?
- Can children recover?
- What can adoptive parents do to help children recover?
- How does therapy work?

Presentation

SLIDE Neglect and abuse

- *Intentional and unintentional abuse have the same impact on the child*
- *Children with disabilities are more vulnerable*
- *Certain forms of ill-treatment may be more subtle, but the impact on the child may be just as severe*
- *Neglect and abuse during the first two years have striking and long-lasting impacts*
- *Similar experiences may be perceived differently by different children, depending on previous experiences, resilience, etc.*
- *Higher incidence of attachment problems among children who have experienced neglect or abuse.*

(Erickson and Egeland, 1996)

Exercise

Tina's story

Read out *Tina's story*, below (and provide the handout). This is an account of a neglectful mother of three (Horwath, 2009).

Now ask participants to take the role of either the five-month-old baby, the seven-year-old son or the 14-year-old daughter and write a day's diary in the voice of that child. Allow them 10 minutes to write. If sitting at tables, each group should ensure that at least one member of their group writes about each of the children. If there are any participants who have difficulty in writing, ask them to find a partner so that they can express their ideas together. After about 10 minutes, invite participants to read out their stories to each other in small

Preparing to adopt

groups. Afterwards, extend the exercise by:

1. asking participants what the risk factors are for each child;

2. asking participants how they think the two younger children's previous experiences might impact on them in terms of what they would expect from their adopters;

3. discussing the likelihood that the 14-year-old girl may be at risk of getting pregnant and following in Tina's footsteps.

Write responses on the flip chart.

HANDOUT

Tina's story

Tina is a 30-year-old mother of three children – Paula, aged 14, Stephen, aged seven years, and John, aged five months. She has a partner, Jason, aged 26, who is John's father. Jason and Tina both have a long history of drug use and currently use a variety of drugs including heroin, cannabis and alcohol. Tina says:

'It was Paula's dad who got me into using drugs. It's been so long now, I need it just to stay normal. Jason's in prison at the moment; he just went out one morning last week and he didn't come back. The kids miss him but I've told Stephen he's gone on holiday. Stephen believes anything you tell him.

'If I haven't got any smack when I wake up I can't think straight. I can't bear the kids. I've got to get out of the house, get on the phone, got to score, get the money together for the day. I need £50 a day and it's a full-time job getting it and then always worrying about getting nicked. Paula's really good with the other two; I don't know how I'd manage without her. She's nearly finished school anyway and doesn't want to go any more. She's got a boyfriend, a flashy bloke with lots of money and a car. He thinks Paula should be a model.

'Stephen's old enough to look after himself now. If Paula doesn't do it, his teacher sorts out his breakfast before school and gets him clothes and trainers sometimes after they said the other kids picked on him because he looked such a mess.

'When I've scored and had a few drinks in the evening, I'm a really good mum. We all have a laugh together, me and the kids and Paula's bloke. The other night we stayed up until two in the morning having a drink and a smoke and a laugh – even the baby stayed up. I paid for it the next day, mind. Didn't get up until the afternoon. Stephen gave the baby a corned beef sandwich to eat for his dinner. Said he couldn't find any milk. The baby nearly choked to death. Stephen was crying. He said he'd cut his hand on the corned beef tin as well. He should know better at his age.'

The needs of children

Information for trainers

Highlight the fact that Tina "blows hot and cold" towards the children and that her behaviour is probably erratic and unpredictable. The children will frequently feel unsafe and may well find it hard to trust adults to meet their needs in future.

Participants will probably be thinking in terms of Stephen and John needing to be adopted one day. Remind them that the 14-year-old daughter in the story, with the older boyfriend, could herself become pregnant and give birth to a child whose needs she is unable to meet and who might have to be adopted.

Presentation

What do "neglect" and "abuse" actually look like?

Explain to participants that they will hear the terms "neglect" and "abuse" a lot as they go through the adoption preparation process. But what do these terms really mean? What experiences does a neglected or abused child actually have? The general public hear about cases in the media where children have tragically been murdered, but there are many more cases that are never publicised.

With the help of the following slides, discuss the kinds of neglect and abuse that some children awaiting adoption have experienced.

Invite participants to give examples of the child's experience of: neglect, emotional abuse, physical abuse, sexual abuse. You can give examples yourself if participants are finding this hard. Discuss the effects of parental substance misuse and domestic violence on children.

Go on to discuss mental health issues in parents and how these can impact on the child's experience.

SLIDE Neglect and abuse

- The neglected child
- The emotionally abused child
- The physically abused child
- The sexually abused child
- The child affected by parental substance misuse
- The child affected by domestic violence
- The child affected by parental mental health issues

Preparing to adopt

Information for trainers

You may find the following "prompt" list helpful.

- **The neglected child**: experiences may include lack of food, adequate clothing, sleep, routine, personal hygiene, intellectual stimulation, medical attention, protection and emotional response.

- **The emotionally abused child**: experiences may include being scapegoated, deprived of physical affection, belittled and humiliated, repeatedly moved from significant relationships, overprotected, racially abused or denigrated because of a disability.

- **The physically abused child** may have been shaken, beaten, burned, bitten or have had bones broken.

- **The sexually abused child** may have suffered anything from inappropriate touching and exposure to pornography to full sexual penetration or sexual exploitation.

- **The child affected by parental substance misuse**: if the child's mother was misusing drugs or alcohol while pregnant, the child may have various physical or mental difficulties. If the substance misuse took place after the child was born, this may have resulted in him or her being neglected or abused in the ways detailed above. Research suggests that alcohol or drug misuse vastly increases the likelihood of neglect and abuse. The parents' priorities may be dominated by finding drugs or alcohol and money may be spent on these rather than basic necessities. Children may be scapegoated or shunned by the community if the drug misuse is common knowledge. Altered states of consciousness in the parents may lead to children being unsupervised, neglected or physically and emotionally abused.

- **The child affected by domestic violence**: "domestic violence" includes psychological abuse and threatening behaviour as well as physical and sexual harm. The effects on a child can be direct physical harm (either deliberate or accidental) but also psychological, in witnessing traumatic events such as their parent being attacked. Even if the domestic violence occurs when children are not present, the effect of domestic abuse on the "victim" parent (e.g. depression, preventing children from playing or making any noise in case it "annoys" the perpetrator) can affect them psychologically. Children may live in a constant state of fear, anxiety and guilt. Domestic violence also often contributes to women and children becoming homeless, with numerous moves and disrupted schooling.

- **The child affected by parental mental health issues** may experience inconsistent care, be the subject of the parent's anxieties or delusional thoughts, be denied normal social interaction, and receive little stimulation or response where parents suffer from depression.

Substance misuse, mental health issues and domestic violence have been called "the toxic trio"; a study found that these factors were present in over a third of all cases where children were seriously harmed or died (Brandon et al, 2008).

The needs of children

SLIDE How might neglect affect a child's behaviour?

- Eating disorders
- Stealing and hoarding food
- Inability to accept care
- Demanding or rejecting attention
- Compulsive self-reliance
- Personal hygiene issues
- Destructive of possessions
- Particularly acquisitive of possessions

SLIDE How might emotional abuse manifest itself in a child's behaviour?

- Stealing
- Lying
- Showing no empathy or conscience for hurt done to others
- Low self-esteem
- Inability to make relationships with peers or adults

SLIDE How might physical abuse manifest itself in a child's behaviour?

- Fearful
- Overly aggressive
- Bullying
- Cruelty to animals
- Preoccupation with violence

Preparing to adopt

SLIDE   How might sexual abuse manifest itself in a child's behaviour?

- Soiling and wetting
- Making inappropriate sexual overtures
- Offering indiscriminate affection
- Having fears and phobias, e.g. getting changed, bathing
- Excessive masturbation
- Being "rude"
- Being fearful of relationships

SLIDE   Effects of parental substance misuse

The child affected by parental substance misuse:

- may fail to thrive
- may have behavioural, cognitive and other psychological difficulties
- may be at risk of blood-borne viruses
- may have had their health needs neglected
- is likely to have experienced neglect and/or abuse of various kinds

SLIDE   Effects of domestic violence

- Babies may be physically harmed while they are still in the womb
- Children who have witnessed domestic violence may remain fearful, even with new carers
- Younger children may show anxiety through stomach-aches or bedwetting
- Some children may act out what they have seen and behave in an angry or aggressive way towards parents, siblings or peers

Information for trainers

Where children have lived with domestic violence, even when they are living with new carers where there is no violence, their expectation may be that the violence still occurs without them seeing it. One young boy, who had been with his foster carer for over two years, finally plucked up the courage to ask her: 'When does Peter (the foster father) hit you, then?'

The needs of children

SLIDE Mental health issues in parent(s)

- May affect parent's ability to care for the child (e.g. depression may lead to neglect)
- May put the child at risk of harm
- Parent may at times be frightened or frightening
- Parent's delusional thinking may involve the child
- Parent may fear harming the child, or say they are going to harm him

Information for trainers

Parent's mental health issues

- Mental health problems *may* seriously impede parent's ability to care for children
- Risk to the child is widely variable
- Impact on each child in the family should be assessed
- Mental health problems fluctuate over time
- Other problems possible, e.g. poverty, social isolation, inadequate housing

SLIDE Parental mental health issues: the impact on the child

- At times, may be wary or afraid of parent
- At times interaction may be inappropriate
- The child may have to care for himself or take on care for younger siblings
- Parent's symptoms may impact on the child, e.g. school attendance, friendships, social life
- Parent may express intention to harm the child

SLIDE Parental mental health issues: delusional thinking

- Anxious parent may express obsessional thoughts that the child may come to harm
- Depressed parent may express feelings that the world is unfit for the child to live in
- The child may have negative meaning to the parent, e.g. because of circumstances around conception or birth
- The child may be central feature of parent's delusional thinking

Preparing to adopt

Exercise

Who's looking at you?

Ask participants to stand in a circle, facing the centre, to play a game. Tell them you would like them to make eye contact with any other member of the circle and then to swap places with this person; you would like them to do this five times in succession with different people.

Say "go" and start the game. When they have all swapped five times, ask them to do it one more time.

Discuss with the group how this exercise made them feel. Some people may say it made them feel anxious in case no one looked at them; they may reflect on how uncomfortable it feels when you are looking at someone but they don't notice you looking. Also ask them how it felt when they thought the game was over, and then they found they had to start again. Some may say they felt initially relieved it was over, then slightly anxious all over again.

Eye contact is fundamental to the way human beings relate to each other. It can be upsetting and uncomfortable to be with people who don't "see" you. Many children who need adoption have had the experience of feeling "invisible" in their birth families.

Presentation

How trauma affects attachments and brain development

Refer briefly to the importance of attachment (which is dealt with more fully in the module *Children's development and attachment*). Remind participants or briefly explain why attachment is so vital, and why neglect can lead to failure of attachment.

Information for trainers

Babies are totally dependent on their relationship with their caregiver for their survival. Without an adult who is committed to care for them, they could die. So it is vital for babies to have a secure attachment relationship that is safe and nurturing. A good attachment experience with a carer who is closely attuned to their needs is extremely important for the baby to develop feelings of trust and security.

If care is not forthcoming or it is erratic, the baby's needs go unmet and this represents a serious threat to the baby. The baby will not develop the ability to regulate stress and his brain development will be compromised. This is **developmental trauma**.

Some children do develop the ability to regulate stress in babyhood but then, at a stage when they are able to process their feelings, they are exposed to terrifying events. They may

The needs of children

be threatened or fear for their lives or see someone close to them threatened or beaten, for example. Overwhelming fear or horror leads to extreme stress and the body is flooded with massive amounts of stress hormones. These cause major areas of brain function to close down, while other areas become activated and sensitised. This is **emotional trauma**.

Childhood trauma can have a long-term or permanent damaging effect on cognitive functions such as learning and memory, on all major bodily systems, and on emotional and social functioning. In time, the child will adapt to his impairments. But adapting can lead to behaviours and other symptoms of disorder that can be puzzling to other people.

Every aspect of his life is likely to be affected – including his behaviour, how he manages his emotions, his ability to learn and his ability to understand, empathise with and interact with other people and form attachments.

SLIDE Traumatic stress

- External event in which the person is confronted with actual or perceived threat to the life or personal integrity of self or others...

Plus...

- Response to the event includes fear, helplessness or horror

Therefore...

- Trauma is a combination of an external event and an internal experience

Information for trainers

Theory and research about traumatic stress

Like all living organisms we generally have an inbuilt preference for survival; for most of their lifespan, living beings seem to endeavour to stay that way. When confronted with a situation that realistically appears to threaten our continued existence, we have an automatic response that greatly enhances our chances of coming out alive. This is known as the traumatic stress response, and the situations that provoke it are known as traumatic events.

Trauma stress has consequences that can lead to mental health problems. It has therefore been a subject of some interest to the medical profession, and there are a number of diagnostic texts that offer definitive statements about trauma, such as the Diagnostic and Statistical Manual of the American Psychiatric Association. Such definitions lead us to conclude that there are two components to traumatic experience.

First there must be an external event, in which the person is confronted with an actual or realistically perceived threat to the life or personal integrity of self or others. Then there must be a response to the event that includes fear, helplessness or horror. Thus trauma is by definition a combination of an external event and an internal experience.

Preparing to adopt

Take note that the event may have occurred to "self or others"; it is important when looking at the needs of children who have been in situations of domestic violence to recognise that we can be traumatised by witnessing the violation of others. There is some evidence that disorders may be even more common and more severe among those who have witnessed extreme violence, for example, than among the direct victims, however terrible their experience (Harris-Hendrinks et al, 2000, p 26).

(Cairns, 2002, pp 99–100)

SLIDE What is trauma?

A sense of helplessness overwhelms the individual…a sense of being unprotected, of disintegration and acute mental pain. The events are often repeated, frequent, and in a context of anger, rejection, a failure to respond to the core of the child's being.

(Bentovim, 1998)

SLIDE Fear arising from a threat

- A threat may be physical: violence, sexual abuse, neglect
- A threat may be emotional: rejection, abandonment, loss
- Separation from a primary attachment figure represents a threat to a child, even if that person is a source of harm

SLIDE Protective responses

- Hyperarousal – fight or flight response to a threat
- Dissociation – freeze – cutting off awareness of what's really happening

SLIDE Hyperarousal and dissociation

- When adults do not help the baby to regulate stress, the baby will either remain hyper-aroused or will dissociate
- Hyper-aroused children show extreme reactions to stimuli
- Dissociated children show minimal reactions to stimuli
- How might these children be seen or labelled?

The needs of children

Information for trainers

Briefly revisit the normal attachment cycle (or explain it for those who have not already attended the module *Children's development and attachment*) and then go on to explain the disturbed attachment cycle.

Hyperarousal

The hyperaroused child may find it impossible to relax or sit quietly and may be addicted to high-stimulus activities such as computer games or creating tension in people around them.

The child may always be "hypervigilant" – on the alert for risk and danger – and will perceive "neutral" stimuli as threatening. Attention and concentration are both severely reduced by hypervigilance.

Dissociation

Some children "dissociate" in response to their physiological state of high stress arousal. Humans have the ability to filter out certain parts of our experience to prevent us from being overwhelmed by stimuli. In dissociation, as a survival mechanism in the face of an overwhelming threat, the child splits his awareness so that he becomes cut off from his own emotions, as though behind a glass wall. He may seem flat and unemotional and unable to recognise his own feelings, even feelings such as cold, hunger and thirst.

SLIDE Securely attached children

- Receive support and comfort – allows them to calm down after a shock
- Understand that the event is over
- Are able to make sense of what happened
- Do not feel they were responsible or it was because they were bad
- Learn how to regulate their emotions

SLIDE Insecurely attached children

- Trauma reinforces their internal working model: the world is an unsafe place
- Magical thinking: 'It happened because of something I did'
- May remain hyper-aroused or "cut off"
- Are unable to regulate their emotions

Preparing to adopt

- Are filled with a sense of shame: 'Bad things happen to me because I am bad'

Show DVD clips

From the DVD, show the following clips from the *In Brief* series by the Center on the Developing Child at Harvard University (http://developingchild.harvard.edu). (They can also be accessed at www.youtube.com/user/HarvardCenter/videos.)

- The first clip is called *Toxic stress derails healthy development*

Learning to deal with stress is part of human development. Constant activation of the stress response can lead to "toxic stress". You may also wish to show the following clips, from the same source.

- *The Science of Neglect* (5.5 minute clip)

Extensive biological and developmental research shows that significant neglect – the ongoing disruption or significant absence of caregiver responsiveness – can cause more harm to a young child's development than overt physical abuse. Damage can include subsequent cognitive delay, impairments in executive functioning and disruption of the body's stress response.

- *Executive Functioning* (5.5 minute clip)

Children's skills for life and learning – such as inhibitory control, working memory and mental flexibility – are shaped by their early experiences. Their ability to focus, hold and work with information, filter distractions and "switch gears" are all vital if they are to manage well at home and especially in school. For some children, adverse experiences in their early childhood may mean that these tasks are more difficult for them than for their peers.

SLIDE Effects of neglect and abuse

- Children's brains are affected in far-reaching ways by neglect and abuse
- Children's behaviour can be puzzling to adopters
- Children also develop behaviours that represent survival strategies in situations of neglect or abuse
- These strategies may be "imported" into their adoptive family
- Trauma triggers may be outside child's conscious awareness, e.g. something may bring back memory of abuse or the abuser

The needs of children

SLIDE There is hope

The repetitive experience of loving parenting can build attachments and new pathways in the brain.

SLIDE Recovery from trauma

- Try to create a sense of calm and safety
- Gentle routines and clear rules
- Nurturing
- Individual time with child
- Allow child to express feelings safely
- Acknowledge the child's distress
- Calm with soothing activities
- Give limited choices
- Allow child time to change internal working model

Share with participants the following anecdote to demystify what "therapeutic parenting" looks like.

A five-year-old boy was on his fourth foster placement – the first three had disrupted due to his behaviour. One of his issues was mealtimes. On the first evening with his carer, she made their evening meal, put the plates on the table and went to sit down at the table. He grabbed the plate, got under the table and sat there eating with his hands. Ask participants what they think happened next.

What happened was that the carer got her plate and cutlery and sat under the table with him to eat her meal. They continued like this for a few weeks until gradually they could sit at the table together. Tell participants this is a perfect example of therapeutic parenting.

Show DVD clip

Show the clip in which experts discuss the effects of neglect and abuse, and how parents can help children to overcome this.

Preparing to adopt

Presentation and group exercise

Helping children through your day-to-day care

The following presentation and exercise are based on Schofield and Beek's (2014) work on the "Secure Base" model, which includes five important parenting dimensions (this was briefly mentioned in Stage One).

Ask participants to join together in small groups of three or four people.

Explain that adoptive parents can do a lot to make the child feel secure by the little things they do as part of their everyday care for the child.

Outline the Secure Base model using the first two slides below.

SLIDE The caregiving cycle

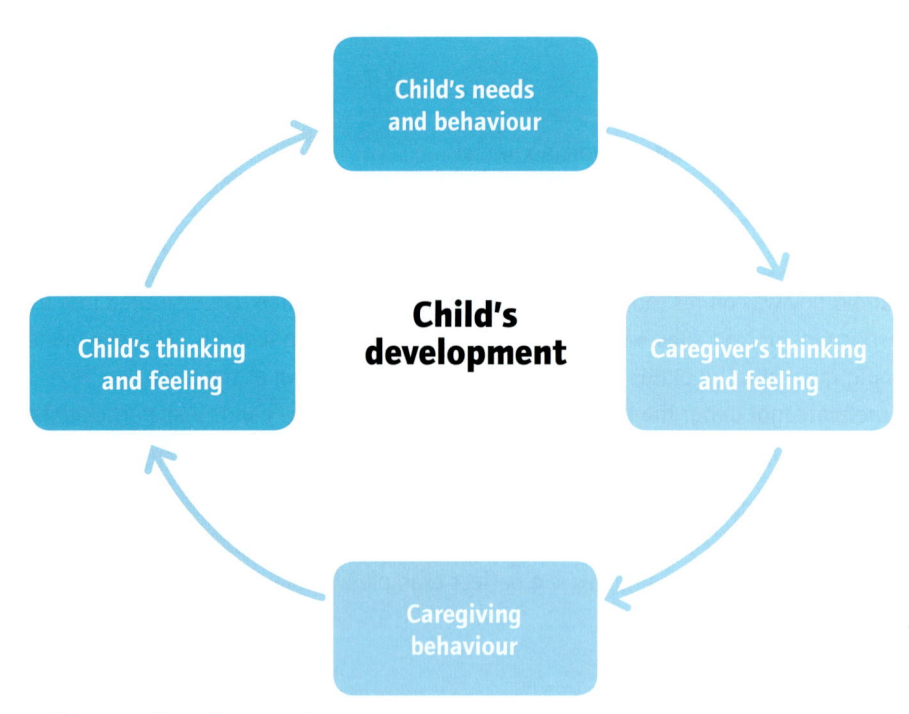

```
            Child's needs
            and behaviour
                  
  Child's         Child's        Caregiver's thinking
  thinking and    development    and feeling
  feeling
                  
            Caregiving
            behaviour
```

Information for trainers

The process of changing children's minds and behaviour through therapeutic caregiving begins in the mind of the caregiver. The ways in which a caregiver *thinks and feels* about a child's behaviours will determine his or her own *parenting behaviours*. Parenting behaviours convey certain messages to the child. The child's *thinking and feeling* will be affected by these messages, and there will be a consequent impact on his or her *behaviour and development*.

The needs of children

SLIDE The Secure Base Model

```
                    AVAILABILITY
                   helping the child
                        to trust

  FAMILY MEMBERSHIP                    SENSITIVITY
    helping the child                helping the child
        to belong                    to manage feelings

                      SECURE BASE

      CO-OPERATION                      ACCEPTANCE
     helping the child                building the child's
      to feel effective                  self-esteem
```

Information for trainers

These five dimensions of parenting – **availability, sensitivity, acceptance, co-operation and family membership** – combine and interact with each other to create the secure base that is essential for the child's healing and development. Over a number of years, Gillian Schofield and Mary Beek researched and developed this "secure base" model of therapeutic caregiving, which has its roots in attachment theory.

Availability

It is important for the caregiver or parent to convey a strong sense of being physically and emotionally available to meet the child's needs, whether they are together or apart. From this secure base, the child begins to trust that they are safe and that their needs will be met warmly, consistently and reliably. Anxiety is reduced and the child gains the confidence to explore the world, safe in the knowledge that care and protection will be available in times of need.

Sensitivity

This is about responding sensitively and helping the child to manage feelings and behaviour. It refers to the caregiver's capacity to "stand in the shoes" of the child, to think flexibly about what the child may be thinking and to reflect this back to the child. The reflective, "mind-minded" caregiver also thinks about their own feelings and shares them sensitively with the child. The child thus learns to think about their own feelings, as well as the thoughts and feelings of others, and is helped to reflect on, organise and manage their behaviour.

Preparing to adopt

Acceptance

This is about accepting the child and building self-esteem. All caregivers need to give the message that the child is unconditionally accepted and valued for who they are, for their difficulties as well as strengths. This forms the foundation of positive self-esteem, so that the child can experience themselves as worthy of receiving love, help and support, and be able to deal with challenges and setbacks.

Co-operation

This is about co-operative caregiving and helping the child to feel effective. The caregiver needs to think about the child as a separate person, whose wishes, feelings and goals are valid and meaningful, and who needs to feel effective. The caregiver therefore looks for ways of promoting the child's capacity to make choices (within clear boundaries) but is also working to co-operate with the child wherever possible. This helps the child to feel more effective and competent and able to compromise and co-operate.

Family membership

This is about helping children to feel they belong and including them, socially and personally, as a family member. An adoptive parent needs to help the child establish an appropriate sense of connectedness and belonging to their birth family as well as their adoptive family. The child who is likely at times to feel uncertainty and have divided loyalties can then be helped to develop a comfortable sense of belonging to both families.

Now show the slides *Availability*, *Sensitivity*, *Acceptance* and *Co-operation*. Each time, ask the participants (in small groups) to come up with ideas and suggestions about:

- What patterns of behaviour might children show if they have not had the care they should have had in that particular dimension?
- Parenting strategies and *practical* ways in which adoptive parents could convey the relevant positive messages to the child on a day-to-day basis.

Each small group should consider children in *one* of the following age groups:

- Babies and toddlers up to 18 months
- Children from 18 months to four
- Children aged from five to 10
- Adolescents

After each slide/discussion, ask for each group to feed back two or three of their ideas.

We include some suggestions after each slide.

The needs of children

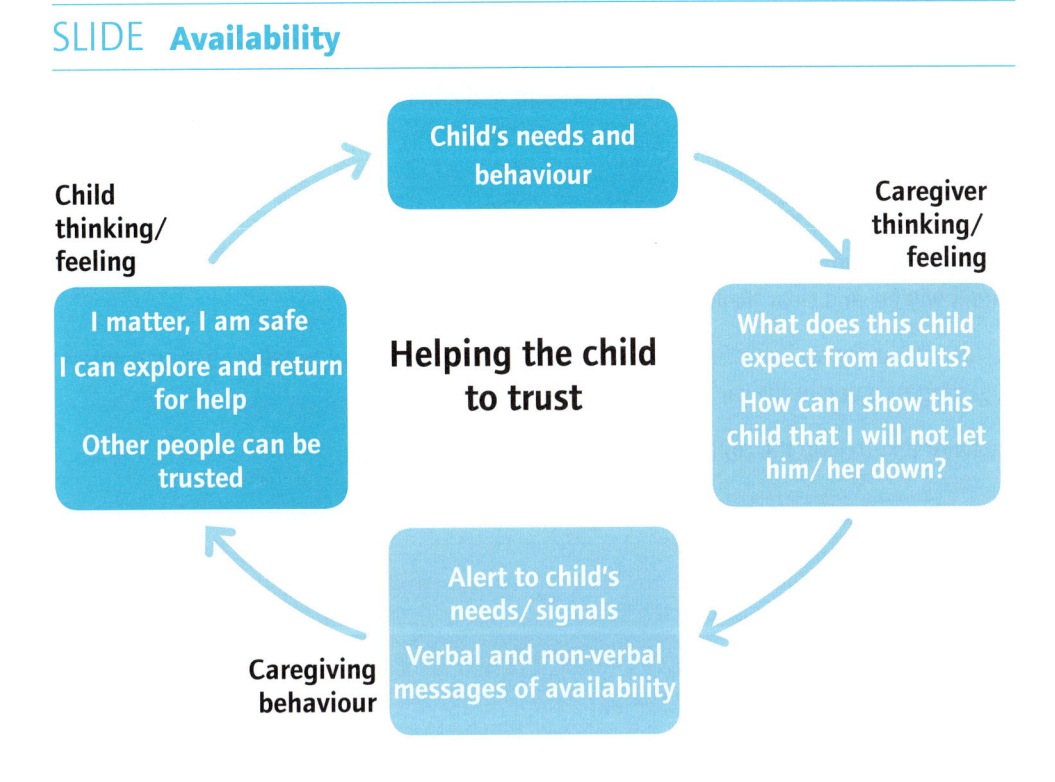

SLIDE Availability

Child thinking/feeling → Child's needs and behaviour → **Caregiver thinking/feeling**

- Child's needs and behaviour
- What does this child expect from adults? How can I show this child that I will not let him/her down?
- Alert to child's needs/signals. Verbal and non-verbal messages of availability
- I matter, I am safe. I can explore and return for help. Other people can be trusted

Caregiving behaviour

Helping the child to trust

Information for trainers

How might children behave when they have lived with adults who have been unavailable, rejecting, unpredictable or frightening?

Children sometimes deny their real feelings of vulnerability because they have had to develop this as a coping strategy with previous carers. So their behaviour may be misleading or confusing for adopters. Examples of child behaviours:

- A baby may be anxious and unsettled.
- A child doesn't run to an adult when she has hurt herself.
- A child may keep adults at a distance and reject their approaches.
- A child may be wary of showing his needs and feelings.
- A child may be very self-reliant and reject offers of help, e.g. puts herself to bed.
- A child may be anxious and attempt to keep adults close by.
- A child may be clingy and "whiney".
- A child may be emotionally demanding.
- A child may be controlling ('I don't trust you to help me so I need to stay in control').

Preparing to adopt

Some approaches for helping children to build trust

- Choose activities that the child is likely to accept and enjoy.
- Establish predictable routines around mealtimes, getting up and going to bed.
- Ensure the child always knows where to find you when you are apart.
- Manage separations carefully, with open communication about why it is happening, how long it will be, and clear "hellos" and "goodbyes".
- Be "unobtrusively available" if the child is anxious but finds it hard to talk or accept comfort (e.g. suggest a ride in the car).
- Phone or text to help the child know you are thinking about him.

SLIDE Sensitivity

Helping the child to manage feelings

- Child's needs and behaviour
- Caregiver thinking/feeling: What might this child be thinking and feeling? How does this child make me feel?
- Caregiving behaviour: Helping the child to understand, express and manage feelings appropriately
- Child thinking/feeling: My feelings make sense and can be managed. Other people have thoughts and feelings

Information for trainers

How might children in that age group behave if they have lacked consistent adults who can see the world from their point of view and provide comfort and reassurance? These children may find it hard to manage their feelings and behaviour.

Some examples:

- A child may be volatile, easily becoming angry or despairing.
- A child may show very little emotion, fearing that their intense feelings and behaviours could become overwhelming to them or to their caregivers.

The needs of children

- A child may have difficulty understanding their own emotions – particularly mixed emotions.

- A child may have difficulty understanding other people's emotions (children and adults) so may fall out with their friends or be socially excluded.

- A child may find it hard to experience joy or excitement or anticipation.

- A child may have difficulty recognising sensory signals, for instance, that they are too hot, too cold, hungry or even in pain.

Examples of parenting behaviour associated with helping children to manage feelings and behaviour

- Naming the child's feelings ('You seem to be upset'; 'I am cross with myself for doing that').

- Using stories and toys to reflect on the emotions and feelings of the characters and help the child develop empathy.

- Mirroring and containing feelings (e.g. a caregiver may mirror a child's distress and say 'Oh, poor you!' and then offer a soothing remark and reassurance).

- Helping the child to pause for thought.

- Acknowledging mixed feelings.

- Modelling the expression of your own feelings – demonstrating to children that feelings don't have to spiral out of control and that minor rifts in relationships are normal and can be repaired.

SLIDE Acceptance

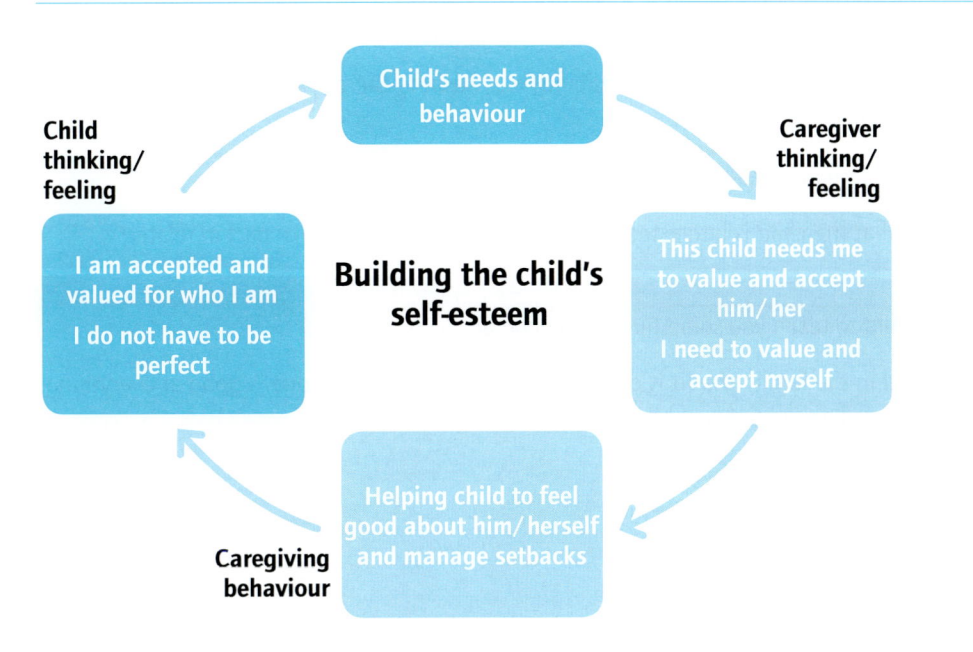

Building the child's self-esteem

- Child's needs and behaviour
- Caregiver thinking/feeling: This child needs me to value and accept him/her. I need to value and accept myself
- Caregiving behaviour: Helping child to feel good about him/herself and manage setbacks
- Child thinking/feeling: I am accepted and valued for who I am. I do not have to be perfect

Preparing to adopt

Information for trainers

From the moment of birth, good parents show with loving words, gestures and tones of voice that the baby is accepted unconditionally, loved, lovable and a subject of interest, value and concern. Babies and children who have not felt accepted and loved will have a damaged sense of self-worth.

How might children in that age group be if they have low self-esteem?

- Feeling unloved.
- Feeling unsure that they are fundamentally "good".
- Fearing that they will not be cared for if they are "naughty".
- Reluctant to take risks – in learning, in relationships.
- Trapped in a negative cycle – they behave in ways that invite negative responses, which are at least predictable. They expect failure and rejection and behave in ways that are likely to produce this outcome.

Examples of parenting behaviour associated with helping children to manage feelings and behaviour

Sensitive caregivers create situations in which their children can feel a sense of achievement, accomplish tasks, receive praise and feel special.

- Play games with a baby and provide toys that create a sense of achievement.
- Ensure the child's heritage is celebrated within the home.
- Use dolls, toys, games and books that promote a positive sense of the child's ethnic, religious and cultural background.
- Giving the child a small task or responsibility, e.g. washing the car, and praising him when he manages it.
- Celebrate his small successes, e.g. doing well in a test or event at school.
- Find out what the child is interested in and help him pursue it or take part in related activities.
- Ask the child to teach you something he is good at.
- Model, within the family, that it is okay not to be perfect, that "no one is good at everything but everyone is good at something".

The needs of children

SLIDE Co-operation

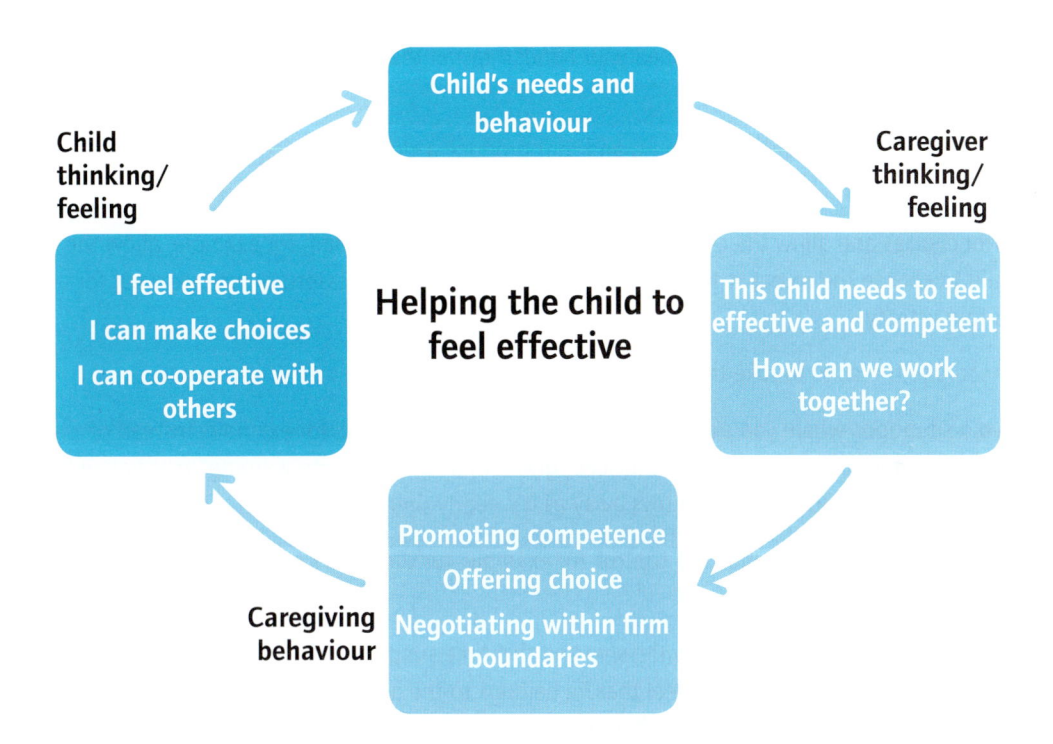

Helping the child to feel effective

- Child's needs and behaviour
- Caregiver thinking/feeling: This child needs to feel effective and competent. How can we work together?
- Caregiving behaviour: Promoting competence, Offering choice, Negotiating within firm boundaries
- Child thinking/feeling: I feel effective, I can make choices, I can co-operate with others

Information for trainers

Sensitive parents view their babies and children as separate individuals who have free will, thoughts, feelings and intentions of their own. They do not, as a rule, interfere abruptly or impose their will on the child – they aim to achieve a co-operative alliance that helps the child to feel effective.

Some birth parents of children who need adoption may have been over-intrusive, harsh or controlling; some may not have been firm enough, allowing children to exert inappropriate control or influence in the family. In some instances, the care system itself can leave children feeling powerless and ineffective. A child with disabilities may also feel powerless and frustrated, if he or she is not helped to make choices and feel competent.

How might children in that age group behave if they have been made to feel ineffective?

- Passive and unresponsive.
- Unable to make choices.
- Some may respond by becoming very controlling themselves – over adults, their peers or their environment.
- Find choice and compromise difficult.

Preparing to adopt

Some parental strategies that can help

- Use co-operative language wherever possible. For example: 'Would you like to come and have a sandwich after you've washed your hands?' rather than 'Wash your hands before you eat your sandwich'.

- Find shared activities the child enjoys and that produce a clear result, for example, baking cakes.

- Offer choices and allow the child to make some decisions for himself, for example, allow the child to choose the cereal at the supermarket, what to have for dessert, or what to wear for a certain activity.

- Encourage the child to take the lead in play and activities.

- Avoid situations where you abruptly impose your will on the child, for example, instead of suddenly announcing that it is time for bed, give him a "three-minute warning" that you will have to stop playing and put the toys away as it's nearly time for bed.

- If you have to intervene and take control, for example, for the child's safety, use humour and diversionary tactics.

Finally, show the slide *Family membership* and this time simply ask the groups to suggest some ways of helping a child to feel that he belongs to the adoptive family and some ways of helping him to manage the fact that he is also a member of his birth family.

SLIDE Family membership

Helping the child to belong

- Child's needs and behaviour
- Caregiver thinking/feeling: This child is part of my family and also connected to their birth family
- Caregiving behaviour: Verbal and non-verbal messages of connection to both families
- Child thinking/feeling: I have a sense of belonging / I can feel connected to more than one family

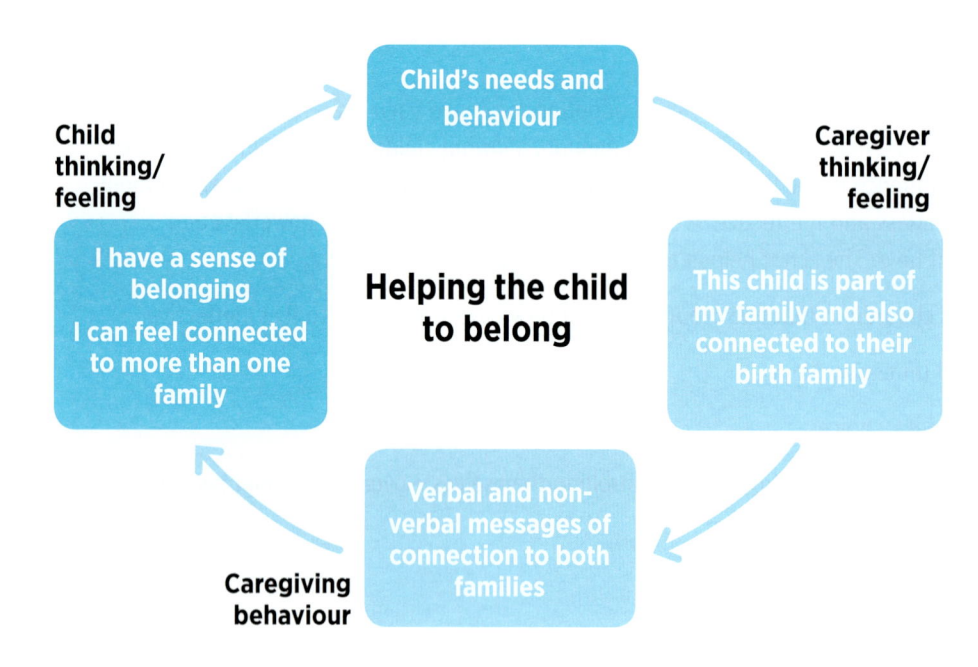

The needs of children

Information for trainers

Family membership becomes an inherent part of a person's identity. Adopted children are members of more than one family.

We will look more closely at issues around the birth family and contact with the birth family in another module, *Telling, contact and social networking*.

You may well find the participants mainly focus on ways in which they can help the child feel he belongs to the *adoptive* family. That is fine at this stage – but you should explain that you will look in more depth at the child's relationship with the birth family in the module *Life as an adoptive family: learning to live together*.

How to help a child feel they belong in your family

- Family celebrations.
- Allow the child to choose how to decorate their own room, choose their duvet cover, etc.
- Explain to the child how your family works – its routines and expectations.
- Accommodate what the child is used to, to help him feel more comfortable, e.g. meals and bedtimes.
- Use photos to build a family story.
- Talk about what you will do together in the future.

How to help a child feel they belong to the birth family

- Develop or build on the child's life story book.
- Display photographs of people from the child's birth family wherever the child would like to put them up.
- Where there is an arrangement for direct or indirect contact, recognise its value and long-term significance for the child's identity needs.
- Talk with the child about being a member of more than one family.
- Help the child think about/talk about the inevitability of mixed feelings.
- If necessary, and with the child's permission, talk to the teacher about issues that may disturb the child if raised in the classroom (e.g. making a Mother's Day card, doing a family tree). Help others outside the immediate family circle to be aware of the child's task in managing their multiple loyalties/families.

Preparing to adopt

Presentation

Attending: providing the child with positive attention

Explain that you want to share with the group one more simple technique that has proved helpful in improving self-esteem and reducing difficult behaviour in children. (This is adapted from Pallett *et al*, 2008.)

"Attending" is a way of providing positive attention to children. It means getting down on the floor next to the child while they play and giving them dedicated one-to-one attention – but by simply commenting on what they are doing rather than by directing their play.

Attending is a non-threatening way of getting alongside a child and positively supporting their spontaneous play. Attending can be immensely powerful, particularly for children who are not used to receiving much positive attention.

SLIDE Attending: how it's done

- Child-led – follow and imitate the child's behaviour
- Non-directive – notice and describe what the child is doing
- Be sensitive to the child – let him choose the toy and move on when he wants to
- Observation – let the child use their imagination
- Positive – make positive comments, ignore minor misbehaviour

SLIDE How it's *not* done

- **Don't** ask the child questions – they are distracting
- **Don't** teach
- **Don't** direct the child's play
- **Avoid** over-structured or competitive play such as board games

Information for trainers

Suitable toys that lend themselves to creativity and imagination are, for example, dolls, cars, Lego, building bricks, paints or a farm set. The adult should simply sit beside the child and watch what he or she is doing and provide a kind of "descriptive commenting" – 'You've put the red car next to the green one. Now you're making the green car go into the garage.'

The needs of children

Adults should resist the urge to start "improving" what the child is doing, making suggestions or imposing their own ideas. It should be led by the child, and the adult should enter the child's world.

Ideally, the adult should try to do this for a short time – say 10 minutes – each day. It has been found to have surprisingly powerful positive effects. The child probably won't want the attending to stop, so it is best if the adult can give a couple of minutes' notice that it's coming to an end but promise that they will do it again later or the next day.

The benefits may not be obvious at first but it is worth persevering – many carers have been amazed at the changes in their children's behaviour when they have started attending regularly.

Exercise

Attending

Part 1:

- Ask the participants to work in pairs: one should play the part of the "adult" and the other the part of the "child", then they should change roles.
- The "child" selects toys or items to draw with out of a box, and plays or draws for two minutes.
- The "adult" takes part in an intrusive manner, making a lot of comments and interventions.
- They change roles.
- Pairs feed back on how it felt as the "child" and as the "adult".

Part 2:

- Again, the pairs take it in turns to be the "child" and the "adult".
- The "child" selects toys or items to draw with out of a box, and plays or draws for two minutes.
- The "adult" focuses on what the child says or does with curiosity and interest.
- The "adult" makes empathic comments – 'you have drawn a circle', 'you are putting a roof on the house'.
- The "adult" does not suggest, praise, teach, direct or take control.
- Participants feed back on how it feels when attending is done well.

Preparing to adopt

Presentation

Building resilience

Start with a group quick-think: what do people understand by the term "resilience"? They will probably think in terms of "strength", "bouncing back" after loss or failing at something, and successfully coming through difficult experiences and circumstances, such as bullying.

SLIDE Resilience

- The ability to survive and thrive under difficult conditions
- Different from "coping"
- Individual and social factors contribute
- A strong sense of identity enhances resilience

Information for trainers

The slides and information about resilience are drawn from the work of Kate Cairns (Cairns and Fursland, 2008).

Resilience is not the same as coping. When we "cope" with difficulties or changes in our lives, we survive them but at a cost – for instance, we may use alcohol as a crutch, avoid certain situations or vent our feelings on others in inappropriate ways. When we are resilient, we find ways of dealing with difficulties that allow us to continue to develop our full potential.

Factors at the individual level that affect a child's resilience include the child's own personal strengths, skills and attributes. Social factors include support from others in the child's network, including adopters, teachers and other school staff, therapists and leaders of activity groups or faith groups.

SLIDE The six domains of resilience in childhood

Factors that increase resilience can be organised into six domains:

- Secure base
- Education
- Friendships
- Talents and interests

The needs of children

- Positive values
- Social competencies

A secure attachment is the most stable and reliable foundation for resilience.

(Daniel and Wassell (2002) cited in Cairns and Fursland, 2008)

Information for trainers

A child can be more or less resilient in these various domains. For example, he may be doing well at school but have few friendships; or he may be struggling academically but be socially very competent and excel in talents and interests outside school.

Remind participants that they have learned about how to provide a secure base for a child (Schofield and Beek's "secure base model", which was covered in detail earlier). Other key people in the child's network can also play an important part in promoting resilience in the child.

Exercise

Promoting resilience

Ask participants to work in small groups. Ask each group to select one child from the seven children featured in the scenarios in the exercise, *Origins of challenging behaviour in children* (see Module 9). Focusing on this one child, ask them to think of *practical* ways in which they could:

- promote the child's resilience;
- engage others in promoting the child's resilience.

Ask the groups to feed back their thoughts to the larger group.

Information for trainers

If it is not suggested by participants, point out that for some children, birth relatives can be a source of resilience (e.g. a relationship with a birth brother or sister in another adoptive placement; a birth grandparent). Other people outside the immediate family, such as adoptive grandparents, aunts and uncles and former foster carers can play an important role too.

A teacher, teaching assistant, sports coach, dance teacher, music tutor, leader of a youth organisation or someone from the child's church or other faith community could take a special interest in the child and encourage his progress. Local sports, cultural and leisure

Preparing to adopt

organisations, clubs, classes and activities can all offer opportunities for a child to discover and pursue his talents and passions, which will enhance his resilience.

Presentation

Therapeutic intervention as part of post-adoption support

Explain that sometimes a child's emotional and behavioural difficulties are such that the kind of therapeutic strategies we have discussed so far in the module are not sufficient on their own. Some adopters and their children need and benefit from therapeutic help from a professional outside the family.

Information for trainers

Many different therapies are used in post-adoption support. They all aim to get you to the same place, but will take you there by different routes. Suggest that effective interventions in post-adoption support are those which include the parents as equal partners.

Sometimes – if the situation is very intense – it might be helpful for the child to have individual therapy (from someone with experience in attachment and developmental issues and post-abuse work) and for the parents to have consultation.

These are the most common interventions in post-adoption support. Parents sometimes source a therapist for themselves and this may become more common in the future when direct payments or personal payments are available. Some CAMHS (Child and Adolescent Mental Health Services) can provide therapists but availability is variable and CAMHS has increasingly moved to a consultation model.

SLIDE Some therapies

Expressive arts

- Art, music, drama therapies
- Play therapy

Psychotherapy

- Counselling
- Psychoanalysis
- Play therapy
- Family therapy

The needs of children

SLIDE More therapies...

Family therapy

- Systemic
- Filial
- Dyadic developmental therapy (this is a psychotherapeutic treatment method for families that have children with emotional disorders including attachment disorders. Originally developed by psychologist Daniel Hughes.)

Behaviour therapies

- Parenting skills groups
- Cognitive behavioural therapies
- Theraplay

Information for trainers

What is non-directive play therapy?

A child's behaviour may be causing stress or difficulties to him or herself or others. They may be showing their feelings in behaviour rather than in words. A child who is frightened or distressed or angry about his experience of life might show it in ways that do not seem to make sense to those who care for him or her. Non-directive play therapy can help a child express those feelings and make sense of them in some way.

This is a therapeutic approach to helping troubled or distressed children, using play. It offers an opportunity for children to explore painful feelings, and understand distressing or traumatic experiences or situations that they may or may not be able to recall in words.

Children use the play room in any way they choose (with due regard for safety). Toys and equipment are selected to enable a child to explore issues that are important to them. They are enabled to use their experiences in the play room – including the relationship with the therapist – to understand and resolve their difficulties.

What is filial therapy?

Filial therapy grew out of the work of non-directive play therapists in the US as a structured treatment programme for children with emotional problems.

Filial therapy addresses the emotional needs of children in the same way as non-directive play therapy, but uses one or both parents or carers as the "agents of therapeutic change". Through teaching, role playing, and observing sessions, a qualified play therapist with the necessary additional training supervises the parent as they hold special play sessions with the child.

Preparing to adopt

What is Theraplay®?

Theraplay® is a method of enhancing attachment, engagement, self-esteem and trust in others. It is based on the natural patterns of healthy interaction between parent and child. It is personal, physical, engaging and fun. Theraplay is a type of parent–child psychotherapy used in a variety of settings.

SLIDE Aims of therapy, for the adult

- Increase understanding of child development
- Develop increased understanding of own child
- Value emotional wellbeing and self-esteem
- Learn new skills
- Develop self-confidence as adults
- Increase feelings of warmth/trust towards child
- Reduce frustration

SLIDE Aims of therapy, for the child

- Express feelings to better convey needs
- Develop problem-solving skills
- Reduce problematic behaviour
- Be heard
- Make better choices and learn to take responsibility
- Increase trust in parents
- Increase self-confidence and self-esteem

SLIDE Key questions

- Has the therapist had experience and training in post-abuse trauma and looked after children work?
- What types of therapy does he/she specialise in?
- Is the therapist qualified or certified by approved bodies?

The needs of children

Information for trainers

Much of the therapeutic work needed for adopted children lies in the realm of post-abuse work and repair through attuned, sensitive, robust and supported parenting. A therapist undertaking this work should have that awareness and be prepared to work alongside parents as well as with the child.

If the group seems interested in hearing more about choosing a therapist, you could expand on this slide with some more questions.

- What is the quality and length of training the therapist has had?
- Is the therapist supervised by an experienced clinical supervisor and how often?
- How long has the therapist worked with children and adolescents?
- Would the child find the therapist friendly?
- Is the therapist available by phone in an emergency?
- Who will be available to the child during the therapist's holiday or illness or during off-hours?
- Is the therapist willing to meet with you in addition to working with the child?

SLIDE Core objectives of therapy

- Promoting emotion regulation, reflective thinking, parental empathy
- Enhancing behaviour management skills
- Opening family communication – developing a shared family story
- Facilitating social participation – helping the family get a life back!

Presentation by an adopter and DVD clip

This presentation should be given by an adoptive parent who can tell the group about his or her own experience of providing "therapeutic parenting" for an adopted child. Whether or not a professional therapist was involved, the main focus should be on the approach the parent(s) took and the progress the child has made. Allow time for questions.

Show participants the DVD clips in which adoptive parents share their experiences of adoption.

To conclude

Summarise the messages you would like participants to take away from this session. It might go something like this:

Preparing to adopt

Some children have experienced things that no child ever should have to live through. Just hearing about the neglect and abuse that some children are subjected to may have been upsetting and disturbing for you. Children don't come through these experiences unscathed. But with the help of adults (both adopters and professionals) who understand the impact of trauma and have learned how to help, they can recover and adapt to their difficulties. If you go on to adopt a child, you can learn more about this. You could be the one to turn a child's life around.

You may wish to end with the closing exercise from page 26 or another closing exercise of your choice.

Suggested reading for trainers

Schofield G and Beek M (2006) *Attachment for Foster Care and Adoption: A training programme*, London: BAAF

Schofield G and Beek M (2014) *The Secure Base Model: Promoting attachment and resilience in foster care and adoption*, London: BAAF

Smith G (2008) *The Protectors' Handbook: Reducing the risk of child sexual abuse and helping children recover*, London: BAAF

For more information about therapy:

Creative arts therapies: www.mind.org.uk/information-support/drugs-and-treatments/arts-therapies/#.UnEWcPmcedA

Dyadic developmental psychotherapy: www.dyadicdevelopmentalpsychotherapy.org/

Filial therapy: www.play-therapy.com/parents.html

Play therapy: www.bapt.info/whatispt.htm

Theraplay: www.theraplay.org/index.php/theraplay/what-is-theraplay

References

Bentovim A (1998) 'Significant harm in context', in Adcock M and White R (eds) *Significant Harm*, London: Significant Publications

Brandon M, Belderson P, Warren C, Howe D, Gardner R, Dodsworth J and Black J (2008) *Analysing Child Deaths and Serious Injuries through Abuse and Neglect: What can we learn?*, London: DCSF

Cairns K (2002) *Attachment, Trauma and Resilience*, London: BAAF

Cairns K and Fursland E (2008) *Building Identity: A training programme*, London: BAAF/Akamas

Erickson M and Egeland B (1996) 'Child neglect', in Briere J (ed) *The APSAC Handbook on Child Maltreatment*, London: Sage Publications

Harris-Hendriks J, Black D and Kaplan T (2000) *When Father Kills Mother: Guiding children through trauma and grief*, London: Routledge

Horwath J (ed) (2009) *The Child's World: The comprehensive guide to assessing children in need*, London: Jessica Kingsley Publishing

Pallet C, Blackeby K, Yule W, Weissman R and Scott S with Fursland E (2008) *Managing Difficult Behaviour: A handbook for foster carers of the under-12s*, London: BAAF

Schofield G and Beek M (2014) *The Secure Base Model: Promoting attachment and resilience in foster care and adoption*, London: BAAF

Preparing to adopt

MODULE 6

Becoming a parent through adoption

Timing

This module will take approximately three hours, not including a refreshment break.

Setting the scene

- Introduce yourself and explain your role in the agency.
- Remind participants how this module fits into your agency's training programme.
- Refer to housekeeping (e.g. location of fire escapes and toilets, timings of breaks, finish time).
- Remind participants of the ground rules (p 17) and invite them to add any other rules to the list.

What you will need

For the exercise *Considering Children*, for each member of the group you will need to provide photographs and descriptive profiles of children (ideally from your own agency) who are waiting for adoption.

Introductions/warm-up exercise

Choose one from pp 24–26 or use one of your own warm-up exercises.

SLIDE Learning outcomes

The aim of this module is to help you to:

- Think about why you want to adopt
- Think more broadly about the child or children you might go on to adopt
- Consider how you might meet the needs of a child when he or she is first placed with you
- Consider the impact adoption will have on your lifestyle and your family life

Becoming a parent through adoption

Exercise

How and why have you come to the point in your life when you are considering adoption?

This exercise encourages participants to reflect on their motivation to adopt.

Asks participants to discuss, in pairs, the following questions:

- Why do you want to have children?
- What do you look forward to most?
- What three things worry you most about becoming a parent?

Now ask the participants to form into small groups to share their thoughts. Ask each group to highlight three points (for each question above) to feed back to the group as a whole.

Note for trainers

If there are participants present who have not yet met others, be aware and acknowledge that they may find it harder to share this information. Reassure participants that there are no "right" or "wrong" answers. Ensure that no one feels pressurised to share anything they don't want to.

Remind them that adoption is about finding families for children rather than children for families. However, if an adoption is to be successful, it is important that there is compatibility between children and prospective adopters, and that adopting a particular child will be able to provide at least some of the rewards that individual prospective adopters are hoping for. That is where matching comes in.

If anyone seems to have serious worries that they do not feel they can address within the group, suggest that they discuss these with their social worker.

Presentation

Our expectations and the reality

SLIDE Life after placement

- What picture do you have of life as a parent?
- What do you expect of your adopted child?
- Adjusting to the reality

Preparing to adopt

Discuss the following with the group:

- Parenting "fantasies" – what do you expect of yourself, of the child, and what picture do you have of family life with an adopted child?

- However much we might wish it to be the case, the healing power of love alone is not always enough. You can't easily or quickly heal a damaged child.

- Just as the child you eventually adopt may not be the child you have imagined and dreamt of, your day-to-day life with your child won't be as you imagine it either. There will be difficult days, and adoptive parents need to know that they mustn't "beat themselves up" when things get tough.

Explain that participants will explore these questions in more depth with their social worker during the assessment process.

Information for trainers

Every prospective adoptive parent...will hold their own particular fantasies of how they will fulfil their new role. They will have not only their visions of success but also the anticipation of how soon they will achieve this – often much more easily and quickly than will be experienced in reality. Knowledge of the extent of children's past hurts may fuel their expectations of "making these better". Thus, awareness of likely difficult behaviour may be mirrored by their anticipation of understanding fully a child's feelings, concerns and needs and being able to reason with them about appropriate ways of expressing these. The more strongly and deeply such parenting fantasies exist, the more difficult it will be for new parents/carers to deal with the many disappointments they will then face. To the reality of the child's complex emotional responses may be added the bitterness of the new parent's ruined expectations.

For all applicants, a continuing personal re-evaluation of what to expect of themselves as well as the child will be essential, informed by a more realistic adjustment of their preconceptions of parenting with the likely realities of life after placement. Applicants will need to remember there is no such thing as a perfect parent, only a "good enough" one who can admit to their faults, learn from their mistakes, enjoy their successes, and who constantly tries to improve and grow as a parent.

(Beesley, 2010, p 78)

Group quick-think

How can you meet and spend time with children?

This exercise may build on ideas shared in information sessions or initial visits.

Ask participants to come up with examples of ways they spend time with and get to know children. They may have started volunteering in a community setting (e.g. schools, children's

Becoming a parent through adoption

centres, voluntary organisations such as Rainbows and Brownies), spending time with friends and relatives who have children, and so on. Write the suggestions on the flip chart. For those who have not had any of these experiences, what could they now think about doing? Refer participants to the worksheet in their Workbook on which they can jot down their thoughts.

For those who have birth children, explore how much experience that child/ren have of sharing their parents within their home.

Explain the value of being *solely responsible for a child in their own home* to experience the feeling of responsibility and of having their space and time "invaded" by a child.

Show DVD clip and discuss

Show the clip (taken from the Channel 4 film *Find me a Family*) in which prospective adopters undertake exercises to explore their motivation to adopt, their relationships and the kinds of children who would be suitable.

Discuss this with the group.

Discussion of "trial parenting" or child care experience for applicants

- Ask participants if they can think of any way they personally could "borrow" a child (e.g. a niece, nephew or child of close friends) and arrange to be "trial parents".

- Suggest how they might prepare for this hands-on experience and how to gradually progress from short visits to the child spending a weekend at their home. Ask the group to suggest what they might need to consider in terms of setting boundaries, safety issues, etc. (for example, they would need to put in place some health and safety measures around their home, such as locking away any medicines and dangerous substances).

- Explain that they can discuss this further with their assessing social worker, but that they might like to start thinking about it and planning for it now if at all possible.

- Encourage them to make some notes about this on the relevant page of their Workbook.

Note for trainer

Different agencies have different requirements in terms of the child care experience they would like applicants to have had, so you should explain to the group the requirements of your own agency.

Preparing to adopt

Exercise

Considering children

For this exercise (adapted from Cousins, 2010, p 18), provide photographs and separate descriptive profiles of 12 real individual children and/or sibling groups awaiting adoption, from your own agency and/or from *Be My Parent* or *Children Who Wait*. Your photographs and profiles should include a child or children with impairments/disabilities, older children, sibling groups and children of minority ethnic or mixed heritage. There should be a set of these photographs and profiles for each member of the group.

Participants should sit in small groups, with each group sitting around a table. Provide each table with three large cards marked "will accept", "won't accept", "not sure". First, provide the photographs alone and ask each participant to place each photo on one of the cards to denote how they personally would feel about adopting that child or sibling group. Then provide the descriptive profiles (only the texts) and ask them to repeat the exercise.

Then show the participants how the photographs match with the profiles. Check to see if the photographs and texts of each child or sibling group have been placed on the same card (i.e. "will accept", "won't accept", "not sure").

- Discuss with the group how they feel about the reunited profiles – did reading the profiles change their minds either way about the children they had seen in photographs?
- Ask for any volunteers to tell the group how they feel about their own choices.
- Acknowledge the guilt people feel at "rejecting" certain children.
- If there are couples in the group, ask them to check whether or not they put the children in the same categories, and to discuss this with each other when they get home.

Presentation from invited speaker(s)

Children with disabilities

The head of a local special school or someone else with in-depth knowledge of a number of children with impairments, disabilities and/or medical conditions should speak to the group. The speaker should talk about some of the children he or she works with (without identifying them), describing their personalities and interests and how they cope with their medical condition/disability while still enjoying life and making the most of their abilities.

Alternatively, you could invite an adoptive parent of a child with a disability to talk to the group about their child. Or perhaps you could invite two or three young people with impairments or disabilities from a fostering support group or young people's adoption support group (if you have access to one). The young people could do short presentations about their lives and their interests. (They may need to be accompanied by their parents or carers.)

Becoming a parent through adoption

Information for trainers

As you may have found from the preceding exercise, *Considering children*, many prospective adopters are reluctant to consider adopting children with disabilities. But seeing and meeting real children waiting for adoption (for instance, by viewing film clips or meeting them at adoption activity days) allows an opportunity for "chemistry" to happen and for the adopters to respond to a child rather than to a description that focuses on the child's disability. The aim of this presentation is to encourage prospective adopters to see past the stereotypes and to view children with disabilities in a new light.

Hearing from young people with disabilities could be particularly valuable for challenging people's preconceptions about disability.

In the most comprehensive survey of adoption in England ever published (Ivaldi, 2000), prospective adopters, asked hypothetically what "kind of child" they could take, showed that they were three times more likely to accept a child who had been sexually abused than a child with a physical disability, and five times more than a child with a "mental disability" – what today we would call a learning difficulty (see also Ward, 2011). This negative preoccupation with impairment clearly prevents a more holistic view. Efforts and imagination must therefore be directed at the linking stage.

Help prospective families to see the real child

Discussions during assessment about hypothetical children tend towards a generic, stereotyped, problem-focused approach where a more holistic, individual description of a child is lost. This is particularly hazardous for disabled children when the traditional matching methodology is for staff, using profiles, to do the matching...It is arguably more effective if prospective parents are given the opportunity to discover for themselves if they might respond directly to an individual child, whether facilitated through photographs displayed in newspapers or magazines, through videos/DVDs or through actual meetings (placement parties) – methods which give the chance for a more rounded appreciation of the "whole" child.

Any method which allows families to make a more direct connection with a child as a whole person in order to test "chemistry" is to be welcomed.

(Cousins, 2011, pp 20–21)

There are several first-hand accounts written by adopters of children with disabilities in BAAF's Parenting Matters series, so you could recommend that participants read some of these if they would like to find out more.

Discussion

To follow up on the exercise *Considering children* and the previous presentation, ask the participants to discuss (in small groups) whether their initial views about the kind of child they could consider adopting have changed at all since they started the preparation process.

Ask for volunteers to feed back their thoughts to the group.

Preparing to adopt

Exercise

What do you need to be a parent?

Ask participants to think about the skills, knowledge and values you need to be a parent. Arrange this exercise as a carousel so people move from one table to another (one table represents "skills", one "knowledge" and the other "values"). Each table should have a large sheet of flip chart paper, and at each table participants should write their ideas on the sheet. Give everyone pens of the same colour.

Then ask them: what else do you need to be an *adoptive* parent? Provide pens of a different colour and ask participants to use these to add to the sheets the skills, knowledge and values that are specific to adoptive parenting.

Presentation

What do you need to be an adoptive parent?

- Refer to what participants have just written about skills, knowledge and values for adoptive parenting in the previous exercise.
- Discuss the tasks for adopters (below) at different stages of the child's life and their impact on lifestyle.
- Discuss the impact of child's history and circumstances, ethnicity, disability and/or medical condition on the tasks.

Group discussion

Having a child will change your life

Initiate a discussion about the changes in lifestyle that will come with adopting a child.

Ask participants, in small groups, to consider the psychological, social, emotional and practical impacts on their lives. Write the following list on the flip chart and ask participants to consider the impact on:

- your relationship with your partner (if you have one);
- your relationship with your wider family;
- your relationships with your friends;
- your job;
- your social life;

Becoming a parent through adoption

- your home and garden;
- your spare time and hobbies and interests.

Take some feedback – a couple of points per group on each of the above. Then ask the groups for ideas about how they can prepare for some of these changes. Ask them to consider:

- How will you prepare your home and garden for a child (ideas may include decorating a bedroom, use of space, health and safety)?
- How do you think you can ensure that you will still have time for your own hobbies and interests?
- How will you be able to adapt your working life to accommodate the changes?
- How do you think you can maintain your adult relationships, friendships and social life?

Take feedback – a couple of points per group on each of the above. Encourage them to make notes on the relevant page of their Workbook when they get home.

Note to trainers

Adoption means "instant parenthood" and this can be a shock to the system for adopters. Their lives will undoubtedly change and they need to realise that they will need support from other people.

A large part of their lives will be spent on the child's or children's needs – the school run, helping with school work, playing together, family outings, after-school activities, visits to the dentist, children's parties and perhaps contact visits with birth family members or previous foster carers.

Their house is likely to be much more untidy and they will have less time to spend on keeping it clean – how flexible are they about the state of their house?

Prompt them to consider how it might be if the child has disabilities or a medical condition. They will need to accommodate the special equipment and aids the child may need. They may have to make many trips to hospital with him for medical appointments. What about mobility issues? How will they get out and about as a family?

Make the point that when they become parents they may find that there are changes in their friendship group (this often happens in any case when people become parents). Remind the group that, as adopters, they will gain new friends and activities, e.g. they may make more friends, either other adopters or other parents from the child's school, adoption-related events, the child's out-of-school activities and so on.

There is more about the need for adoption support in the module *Life as an adoptive family: learning to live together*.

Preparing to adopt

Sibling groups

With the help of the following slides, discuss the particular joys and challenges of parenting a group of siblings. The adopters quoted in the slides had adopted groups of three or more.

SLIDE Adopting brothers and sisters

Obviously it's a massive life change and experience, but we love the kids to bits, can't imagine life without them and the last year has just gone so quickly…Absolutely no regrets at all.

(A sibling group adopter quoted in Saunders *et al*, 2013, p 70)

I had been a teacher…before this. None of this prepared me for the "full-on" emotional ride that three young children bring. My weight has gone up and down, my sleep habits have changed and my need for adult companionship increased. I am permanently tired even when they are at school.

(A sibling group adopter quoted in Saunders *et al*, 2013, p 66)

Information for trainers

A study by Saunders and Selwyn (2013) interviewed adoption agency managers and staff and 37 adopters of sibling groups. They looked at the adopters' perspectives on how it was working out.

- According to their adopters, the vast majority of the children adopted in sibling groups in the study were making progress and doing quite well or very well.
- Most adopters (68 per cent) reported some difficulties, but almost a third of the adopters reported no difficulties or only a few minor problems.
- The responses from the six adopters who had taken sibling groups of four were particularly positive.
- Some sibling group adopters said it was the hardest thing they had ever done, while others said everything "just felt so right".
- A third of the adopters were always tired, and a quarter said that having the children had put a strain on their relationship.

SLIDE Extended families

- Your parents will become grandparents to your adopted child.
- Your brothers and sisters will become uncles and aunts.
- **How can they help?**

Becoming a parent through adoption

Note to trainers

Extended family members may be very enthusiastic about meeting an adopted child but, for the sake of not overwhelming the child with new people, they may need to be patient and wait until the child has settled in and got to know his or her new parents first. Later on, practical help, such as help with housework or preparing meals, may be very much appreciated, especially if the adopters have a sibling group. In some cases, it may be useful to identify one or two people who are able to offer early support, particularly if adopters have a child/children with special needs or are adopting a sibling group.

Prospective adopters need to consider whether their extended family members are ready to welcome the child into the family or whether they may have reservations (either privately or openly), especially if the child is seen to be "difficult". Transracial adoptions too may raise complex issues in some extended families.

Unconditional acceptance by extended family members is as important to the child and their future as that offered by the adopters if children really are to become a full and permanent part of the wider family network. The child whose birthday is not remembered in the same way, or who is not fully included in the treats or outings offered to any birth children in the family, will inevitably suffer the recurrence of past feelings of rejection.

Ambivalence or dislike of the child's heritage and identity may be either a conscious or explicit factor in the extent to which the child is accepted within certain adoptive families. Where adults in close contact are unable to value the child's heritage, adopter(s) need to consider how they will work actively with those involved concerning their attitudes and promote the child's right to acceptance as a full and valued member of their family.

(Post-Adoption Centre/Talawa, 2008, section 1, p 9)

You may wish to recommend the book *Related by Adoption* (Argent, 2014), a brief handbook which gives grandparents-to-be and other relatives and friends information about how they can support building a new family through adoption and the positive roles they can play.

Adopted children may be seen as being "rescued", which can put them in victim mode, or "lucky" to have been adopted. These attitudes may be communicated at a conscious or unconscious level by family members, friends, community, etc. Adopters need to consider a "script" for introducing children, particularly older children, that respects them and is inclusive. If your agency runs a preparation group for friends and extended family members, make the details available to participants.

To conclude

To sum up, you could say something like this:

Adopting a child is likely to change your life in all sorts of ways. At the moment, you may find it hard to imagine what life will be like with your adopted child or children. You may find that you eventually decide to adopt a child or children who are quite different from what you currently expect or imagine they will be like. For everyone, this new life presents

Preparing to adopt

new challenges, however well-prepared you are. We hope this session has helped you to reflect on some of the changes adoption will bring to your life and your family.

You may wish to end this session with the closing exercise on page 26 or a closing exercise of your choice.

Recommended reading for trainers

Argent H (2014) *Related by Adoption*, London: BAAF

References

Beesley P (2010) *Making Good Assessments: A practical resource guide* (second edition), London: BAAF

Cousins J (2010) *Pushing the Boundaries of Assessment*, London: BAAF

Cousins J (2011) *Ten Top Tips for Making Matches*, London: BAAF

Ivaldi G (2000) *Surveying Adoption*, London: BAAF

Post-Adoption Centre/Talawa (2008) *Supporting Black and Minority Ethnic Children: Attachment and race – a training resource pack*, London: Post-Adoption Centre

Saunders H and Selwyn J (2011) *Adopting Large Sibling Groups: The experiences of adopters and adoption agencies*, London: BAAF

Saunders H and Selwyn J with Fursland E (2013) *Placing Large Sibling Groups for Adoption*, London: BAAF

Ward E (2011) 'Taking the next step: enquirers to National Adoption Week one year on', *Adoption & Fostering*, 35:1, pp 6–17

MODULE 7

Linking, matching and introductions

Timing

This module will take approximately three hours, not including a refreshment break.

Setting the scene

- Introduce yourself and explain your role in the agency.
- Remind participants of how this module fits into your agency's training programme.
- Refer to housekeeping (e.g. location of fire escapes and toilets, timings of breaks, finish time).
- Remind participants of the ground rules (p 17) and invite them to add any other rules to the list.

What you will need

You will need copies of *Me and My Family* by Jean Maye and *My Life and Me* by Jean Camis to show to the participants.

SLIDE Learning outcomes

The aim of this module is to help you to:

- understand how adopters are linked and matched with a child or children
- understand the process of preparing children for adoption
- know what to expect in terms of meeting your child(ren) and having your child(ren) move in
- consider how you can help your child(ren) to settle in
- consider how to support children's identity needs

Introductions/warm-up exercise

Choose one exercise from those outlined on pp 24–26 or use one of your own favourite warm-up exercises.

Preparing to adopt

Presentation

Linking and matching

SLIDE Linking: how does it happen?

There are two ways in which a child and family are linked:

- by social workers cross-matching data (or knowing a particular child) and thinking you may be suitable for that child

- by you responding to information about the child(ren) or meeting them at an event and making an enquiry about them

Information for trainers

Linking and matching

These terms were once used interchangeably but it is more helpful to name them as distinctive processes:

The link *can be described as the initial step in thinking that this family may be suitable for this child: the point when, out of all the families and all the children, the two halves are first placed side by side.*

Links can be achieved through one of two different methods: either through social workers cross-matching data about the child and potential families, or through families themselves responding to information about children (profiles, photographs, videos/DVDs – even through face-to-face meetings in specially arranged adoption activity days) ...

With adopter-led linking:

... the link suggests itself through a response to the child by the adults – often through publications such as Be My Parent or Children Who Wait...With this method, social workers stand back and allow chemistry to play its part. Their skills come in at the next stage – the match.

(Cousins, 2011, p 3)

SLIDE Matching

- Social work staff look carefully at whether *this* child and *this* family are well suited

- Could this or these prospective adopter(s) meet this child's needs?

- Will adopting *this* child give the adopter(s) what they are hoping for?

Linking, matching and introductions

- What support will be needed to make this match successful?
- If it proceeds, the match is considered by the panel and agency decision-maker

Information for trainers

The match *can be described as the outcome of a considered assessment of the potential link by social work staff and eventually the panel and the agency decision-maker. It is a conclusion reached that this child and this family are indeed suited to each other, and that the connection should be formalised. The process of assessing the compatibility of the two parties involves a careful exploration of whether the child's needs could be met by these carers; whether the family's needs could be met by the child; and what supports might be necessary to ensure a long-lasting relationship. No one should doubt the complexity of this process, or the skills required.*

(Cousins, 2011, p 4)

SLIDE Identifying the child's needs

The child's social worker looks at the child's needs in respect of:

- siblings
- implications of past experience
- development
- present functioning and probable future behaviour patterns
- educational needs
- ethnicity
- language
- religion
- contact with birth family and significant others
- health
- geography (location)

SLIDE Taking into account the child's view

If the child is old enough and capable of understanding, the social worker should:

- consult the child about his future

Preparing to adopt

- hear and respect the child's wishes and feelings (without encouraging unrealistic expectations)
- hear what the child thinks about the family identified for him

SLIDE Linking you with a child or children

- When you are approved, the agency agrees with you a written matching agreement
- Your social worker looks for children for whom you might be suitable
- The children's social workers liaise with the agency's family placement team and consider profiles of possible families
- You can also look for possible children
- Your details may be given to a local consortium of agencies
- After three months, your details may be sent to the Adoption Register
- A link will be made between you and a particular child (children)

SLIDE When a link has been made ...

- You receive the Child's Permanence Report (CPR)
- You meet with your social worker and the child's social worker to discuss the link

SLIDE A match is made!

- If everyone agrees to proceed, the child's agency agrees a support plan with you
- The local authority has a duty to give you comprehensive information about the child
- You may be able to meet the child's foster carer, nursery or school teacher
- You may be shown/given a photo, DVD or video
- Possible meeting with the agency medical adviser who can share appropriate information

Information for trainers

- When prospective adopters are approved, the agency must prepare a written matching agreement with them, setting out the matching process and the adopters' role in identifying possible children.

Linking, matching and introductions

- Local authorities have a duty to assess a child's support needs and to make and agree an adoption support plan with prospective adopters when a match is being considered. For example, this might cover any financial support, therapy for the child, training for the adopters and respite care. This will include arrangements for contact.

- Statutory Adoption Guidance 4.24 states that, when considering a match between prospective adopters and a child:

  It is unacceptable for agencies to withhold information about a child and provide a picture that bears little relation to the reality. The information includes the history of any abuse or neglect and/or sexualised behaviour on the part of the child, their history in care, including the number and duration of placements, education and progress (or difficulties), behaviour and comprehensive information about physical and mental health and development and the implications for the future.

  (Department for Education, 2013)

- Prospective adopters are often keen to know if they can see pictures or DVDs of the child at the point of the link or match being made – you should explain your agency practice and the importance of adopters agreeing to keep all shared information confidential.

- Refer the group to the flowchart in their Workbook: *Process for identifying a family after a decision that a child should be placed for adoption.*

Group quick-think

Learning about your child

Ask the group to suggest ways they could learn more about the child they have been matched with (before they meet the child), and write their suggestions on the flip chart. These may include some of the points outlined below.

Information for trainers

Finding out about the child

As an adopter who has been matched with a child, you could:

- *Talk to adults who know the child well (e.g. child's foster carers).*

- *Discuss the Child's Permanence Report fully with social workers.*

- *Ask for a Child/Life Appreciation Day.*

- *Meet significant family members and friends. The agency should have prepared you for the advantages of meeting the birth parent/s even if direct contact may not continue. Many adopters see this as important for the child's future.*

Preparing to adopt

- *Have access to relevant sections of the child's file and relevant documentation, e.g. Personal Education Plan, medical adviser's report.*

- *Talk to foster carers about ways in which they handle any difficulties.*

- *Consider the proposals for contact and whether you are comfortable with them.*

- *Visit the child's nursery or school to talk to staff about the child's progress.*

- *Receive and discuss a proposed written Adoption Support Plan.*

(Salter, 2013, p 35)

There are other people, too, who could provide valuable information to the adopters:

Access to the agency's medical adviser allows the adopters to talk over all medical information and to gain an understanding of what particular aspects of the child's history might mean in the future, for example, where there are concerns about parental drug or alcohol misuse, mental health or hereditary conditions. Health visitors can fill in the developmental details about a young child, especially if the child has any degree of disability or requires special treatment.

It is always helpful for prospective adopters to speak to the teachers of school-age children and to see for themselves the environment where the child has spent a great deal of time. School may be as significant as the foster home, and will certainly be compared by the child with the next one.

(Dunbar, 2009, pp 23–24)

(Explain to the group that they will learn more about contact in the module, *Telling, contact and social networking*.)

Group quick-think

What would you want to know?

Ask the group to suggest questions they would want to ask once a match has been agreed. Write their suggestions on the flip chart. Their suggestions will probably include most or all of the points outlined below in the section on *The Adoption Placement Plan*. Explain that, following a planning meeting, they will be provided with a written adoption placement plan from the child's agency. You could refer the group to the worksheet in their Workbook, *What I would like to find out about the child*, and ask them to jot down their thoughts later.

SLIDE Next steps

- The child's social worker prepares paperwork, including the adopters' PAR, the child's CPR and Adoption Placement Report for the local authority adoption panel

Linking, matching and introductions

- The adoption panel considers the proposed match
- The panel makes a recommendation, advises on contact and adoption support
- The agency decision-maker makes decision
- The child's social worker contacts family, outlines agency's proposals for placement in Adoption Placement Plan
- The adoptive family agrees to Placement Plan
- A Child Appreciation Day may possibly be held
- A meeting is held to plan introductions if not already done at time of Placement Plan
- Possible meeting with birth parents

Information for trainers

A Child/Life Appreciation Day is a day when significant people in the child's life are invited to meet with the adopters to share information about the child. These people could include former foster carers, teachers, health visitors, child minders and former social workers. Family members may be involved too. Those involved will be able to share anecdotes and stories that may not be included in more formal reports. Explain your own agency's practice to the participants.

SLIDE The Adoption Placement Plan sets out:

- Placement order or consent of parent?
- How child and adopters will be prepared for placement
- Date of placement with adopters
- Arrangements for reviewing placement
- Adopters' parental responsibility
- Support services
- Contact arrangements
- Arrangement for life story book/later life letter
- Social workers' contact details

Preparing to adopt

Information for trainers

The Adoption Placement Plan sets out the following:

Content of Adoption Placement Plan – Schedule 5, Adoption Agency Regulations 2005

1. Whether the child is to be placed under a **placement order** or **consent of the parent/guardian**.
2. The arrangements for **preparing the child** and the prospective adopters for the placement.
3. The **date on which it is proposed to place the child** with the prospective adopters.
4. The arrangements for **review** of the placement.
5. **Whether the parental responsibility for the prospective adopters is to be restricted** and if so, the extent to which it is to be restricted.
6. **The support services** to be provided for the adoptive family.
7. **The agency's arrangements for allowing any person contact** with the child, the form of contact, the arrangements for supporting contact and the name and details of the person responsible for facilitating the contact arrangements (if applicable).
8. **The dates on which the child's life story book and later-life letter are to be provided** by the adoption agency to the prospective adopters.
9. Details of **any other arrangements** that need to be made.
10. **Contact details** for the child's social worker, the prospective adopters' social worker and out-of-hours contacts.

A final planning meeting will help everyone involved to understand each other's roles, responsibilities and expectations during the post-placement period. For example, you will want to know:

- the extent to which both social workers will be involved with the child during the placement;
- what contact (if any) the child will have with the birth family;
- if the child will have any continued contact with foster carers;
- what arrangements need to be made with other services (health, education) and who should arrange them; and
- what adoption support services are to be provided and when and how they are to be provided.

(Salter, 2013)

Linking, matching and introductions

SLIDE How will the child or children learn about you?

- From their social worker
- From their foster carers
- From photos, a DVD and/or a book that you put together for the foster carer to show them

Information for trainers

You might like to read out this example of a book prepared by prospective adopters:

One prospective adopter made a family book of photographs showing themselves in each of the rooms of the 'new' house. On each page 'Eddie the Teddy' was hidden somewhere in the picture. On the first day of introductions, the adopters took Eddie the Teddy with them to meet their new child and they wore the same clothes they had worn in the photographs. By reading and re-reading the book to the child, the foster carer ensured that Eddie the Teddy became a firm favourite, as did the adopters!

(Dunbar, 2009, p 10)

Some "talking" books are also now available where adopters can record their own voices and introduce pictures of themselves, their house and their family. This can be especially effective for younger children. Or adopters can make a short DVD about themselves, their home, family and pets, if any.

Introductions

- Briefly outline how introductions usually happen over a period of time, usually between seven and 14 days. Introductions start with the adopters meeting the child(ren) during a short visit to the foster carer's home, and gradually increasing their involvement in the child's/children's care, followed by the foster carers then bringing the child(ren) to the adopter's home for visits, until the child(ren) moves in.

- Point out that the process for a baby will be very different (and probably much shorter) than for an older child or sibling group. Each introduction plan will be unique.

- Explain that, for the child, leaving the foster carers is likely to be difficult. Even if the child wants to be adopted and is excited about meeting the new parents, he is also likely to feel anxious, apprehensive and possibly upset about leaving the foster carers, especially if he has become attached to them.

- Remind the group that leaving the foster home represents another loss for a child who may have already experienced many moves and losses. Even if he has been doing well in his foster home, this move may disrupt him and affect the way he feels and behaves in the adoptive placement.

Preparing to adopt

SLIDE Introductions and moving in

- Child gradually introduced to adopters
- Child moves in with adopters
- Visits from child's and adopter's social workers and reviews of placement
- Decision to apply for adoption order made at child's review
- Adoption Support Plan reviewed and updated as needed
- Adopters make adoption application
- Adoption order is made at court

SLIDE Preparing children

- Adults need to explain to children why they are being moved even though they may be happy and settled
- Adults need to introduce and explain the concept of adoption and what it means
- Children need to be prepared for introductions/placement and what is happening
- Babies and toddlers will not understand
- Also more challenging for children with special needs, e.g. a child who is blind or developmentally delayed

Information for trainers

You might like to ask the group for ideas on how they could ensure that a child who is visually impaired would recognise the adopters from one visit to the next. Here is an example:

Natalie was blind. Her prospective carers always wore the same clothes and watches and jewellery during introductions, the same scent and aftershave lotion. They always brought the same audiotape to play to her and when introductions moved to the new home, the clothes and smells and sounds came too.

(Argent, 2006, pp 46–7)

Group quick-think

Ask the group what they think are the purposes of introductions, then show the following slide.

Linking, matching and introductions

SLIDE Purpose of introductions

- Child and adopters learn about each other first-hand
- Child can make gradual transition from current to future carers
- Adopters become familiar with child's routines
- Adopters and child can begin to build positive attachment
- Current carers can let go, adopters become confident enough to take over

Make the point that introductions are a prelude to placement, and are not in any sense a "trial run". However, that doesn't mean there is no going back. If adopters feel that, once they have met the child, they do not want to go ahead, they can still withdraw. Adopters should be honest with each other and with their social worker if they have doubts, rather than being afraid to admit their true feelings. The introduction period should be reviewed – adopters should be able to ask for more time and adults also need to be aware of the timescale that will best meet the child's needs.

Make the point that introductions should generally be timed to avoid Christmas, birthdays and other festivities and emotionally charged events.

Adopters may need financial support during introductions, for example, if they travel a long way or need to stay in hotels near the foster family. Remind them that this may be available.

Explain that introductions can seem very intense for adopters – they are often spending long periods of time in someone else's home and can also feel they are being scrutinised by foster carers. The more closely they can work with the foster family, the more likely it is that the child will feel he has "permission" to move. Also highlight to adopters that birth children of the foster carers will also be undergoing a process of loss and that it can be helpful to include them in a visit to their home so that they know where the child will be living.

Presentation from a foster carer

An experienced foster carer whom you have invited to address the group should describe how he or she helps prepare children for moving in with their adoptive families. Allow time for questions at the end of the presentation.

Information for trainers

Good foster carers are skilled in helping children prepare for their move.

Children who are securely attached to their foster carer are likely to be bereft, and a child who has been "parenting" younger siblings may not regard an adopter as the person in charge. Foster carers can help to defuse these tensions by properly preparing children to

Preparing to adopt

move to a permanent family, being positive about the adopters, involving them fully in the children's care, and "letting go" of the child when it is time to move them on.

(Saunders *et al*, 2013)

Group quick-think

- Ask participants to close their eyes for a few minutes and imagine they are going to live with a family in another country where they don't speak the language. What aspects of this new life would feel strange to them? What would help to make them feel a bit more comfortable? After a couple of minutes, ask participants to call out their suggestions. (Their suggestions will probably cover communication, food, daily routines, smells, bedtimes, bathing, family and religious rituals, pets and so on.) Write these on the flip chart.

- Draw parallels with how it feels for a child to move in with an adoptive family, and how many things about this new family and environment will feel strange for them. The following presentation will help them think about ways they can make the settling-in period a little easier for the child(ren).

- If it hasn't already been suggested, explain that one of the things that might help is being prepared in advance by knowing something about the family you are going to. As you will have mentioned earlier in this session, some adopters prepare a photograph album or even a short film to introduce themselves, their home and their family to the child who will be moving in with them.

Information for trainers

At this point it would be a good idea to show the group the book *Me and My Family* by Jean Maye. This is an interactive and fun "welcome to our family" book through which adopters can initially introduce themselves to the child, and for the child to work through and record the changes in their lives as they move to their new family. It includes space for drawings, writing and photographs.

Presentation

Introductions for children of different ages

SLIDE Introductions for babies 0–18 months

- They cannot understand change – they can only "feel" it
- May experience loss of usual carers as total abandonment and be distressed

Linking, matching and introductions

- Implications for introductions

Information for trainers

Implications for introductions:

- Create familiar sensory experiences, i.e. how things look, smell and feel.

- Keep the baby in the same routine as in the foster home...There will be plenty of time to make gradual changes later...Adopters should understand that "tuning in" to the child's needs will promote strong attachments far more quickly than trying to impose unfamiliar routines.

- Use the same washing powder so that bedding and clothing feel and smell the same.

- Keep the foster carers in the picture as much as possible; an infant will not understand the reasons for sudden separation.

- Allow the child to grieve, while offering comfort.

SLIDE Introductions for children 18 months–3 years

- May regress to earlier behaviours, e.g. toilet-training, eating, sleep patterns, getting upset easily

- Adopters should retain established routines

- Familiar objects, bedding, favourite toys and clothes will ease transition

SLIDE Introductions for children 3–5 years

- May find new situations threatening

- Change may trigger memories of earlier moves

- Often very interested in books and DVDs provided by the prospective adopters

- May be able to follow a simple calendar outlining waiting time and/or what will happen on each day of introductions

- Foster carer can reassure child, help adopters learn about child

Preparing to adopt

SLIDE Introductions for children 5–10 years

- May feel anxious about hurting their present carers or birth family members
- Foster carers may have ambivalent feelings if bonds are close – glad but sad
- They may need to show the child that he/she has "permission" to form new attachments
- The child also has to cope with a new school, new friends and new community

Information for trainers

The slides are adapted from material written by Dunbar (2009) about children's developmental needs at different ages and the implications for introductions.

Children may not be functioning at the level of their chronological age and people should take account of this in planning. Romaine *et al* (quoted in Dunbar, 2009) observe, when thinking about older children:

There can be a tendency to talk to children about all the good things that moving to a permanent family will bring and avoid any painful ambivalent feelings a child might have. It will be more helpful if children are allowed to express and discuss negative feelings as well as positive ones, to avoid them receiving a message that negative feelings are not valid or acceptable.

(Romaine *et al*, 2009, p 97)

Foster carers can help the child to prepare for introductions by talking about the new family and the new home. They could also give them photographs or put together a memory book to help them remember the foster family and friends they have made there. Some carers remain supportive friends of the new family.

SLIDE Introductions for children with disabilities

- Adopters will need time to feel confident caring for the child's medical and physical needs
- Important to meet with consultants, specialists where possible
- Special considerations for a child with sensory disabilities meeting new parent(s)

Linking, matching and introductions

SLIDE Introductions and placement for siblings

- Some sibling groups may have been living in separate foster homes
- Adopters are usually introduced to all the siblings together
- The plan may specify time to get to know each child individually
- Placing at same time or consecutively? There is no single "right" way
- They can be placed together even if fostered separately
- If children have depended on one another for support, separating them may cause distress
- Consecutive placements can be helpful in some cases

Information for trainers

Placing siblings

Hilary Saunders and Julie Selwyn (2011) carried out research on 37 sibling group adopters, who had adopted three or more siblings. They found that adoption managers thought siblings should usually be placed at the same time to avoid jealousy, suspicions of favouritism or the establishment of a "pecking order". In most cases (92 per cent) siblings were placed simultaneously.

Most adopters thought this was a good decision and ten adopters (27 per cent) insisted that it would not have worked if the siblings had been placed consecutively – they thought that this would have caused anxiety and distress, particularly in cases where one child had acted as parent to the others or they depended on each other for support.

Saunders and Selwyn say that consecutive placements can be helpful when one child or more has very difficult behaviour or when there is a big disparity in children's ages. Careful planning will be needed to ensure that siblings receive individual attention, especially when a baby is involved. For young children, it may be better to avoid overnight stays with adopters before placement.

SLIDE Taking into account children's views

- Introductions need to go at a pace that feels comfortable for the child
- The pace shouldn't be dictated by the emotional needs of the adults
- Adults may need to be flexible about timing
- It's better if child can start a new school at the start of a new term

Preparing to adopt

Exercise

Cultural differences

Ask the participants to divide into small groups. Ask half of the groups to imagine that they are adopting a white child and the other groups to imagine they are adopting a child of mixed heritage. Ask them to consider how they would try to ensure that the child feels as comfortable as possible in his new home.

After participants have discussed this in small groups, ask each small group in turn to feed back one or two of their ideas to the larger group. Continue asking each group to feed back ideas until you have heard them all.

Note to trainers

Encourage the group to think about ethnic, cultural, linguistic and religious issues. Ensure that they consider differences in socio-economic status as well as ethnic differences.

They may consider questions such as: whether the child is used to sitting at a table to eat meals; the type of food the child is used to (e.g. a child may only ever have been given junk food; a child of Pakistani heritage may have been used to food from that region – or not); the type of music the adoptive family listen to, the type of toys they provide and the television programmes they watch at home, and so on. Think about communication issues (including non-verbal communication) and the impact of regional dialects and words and concepts that may be unfamiliar to a child. Think about clothes and personal care, care of the child's hair and so on.

The children who need families are very likely to come from a "different" background from that of their carers and it is essential that applicants understand that at some stage the "difference" will emerge.

(Beesley, 2010, p 177)

Presentation

Matching ... and children's identity needs

SLIDE Child's cultural background

When placing children with adoptive families, agencies are legally obliged to take into account children's needs, wishes and feelings and the importance to the child in their daily life of the following:

- religious persuasion

Linking, matching and introductions

- racial origin
- cultural and linguistic background

SLIDE Ethnicity and matching

- **But...**social workers are expected to avoid "labelling" a child or placing the child's ethnicity above other relevant characteristics (without good cause) when looking for an adoptive family

- Social workers have to strike a balance between finding the best match and finding a family without too much delay

- A prospective adopter can be matched with a child with whom they do not share the same ethnicity, provided they can meet the most important of the child's identified needs throughout childhood

Information for trainers

Where they don't share the child's ethnicity/religion or cultural heritage, what are the tasks for adoptive parents?

- Explain that agencies are expected to take into account children's religious persuasion, racial origin and cultural and linguistic background alongside their other needs, when placing them with adoptive families, but must ensure that this does not mean the child experiences unacceptable delay in achieving adoption. Where possible, it can be in the child's best interests to be placed with families who share these characteristics. Hopefully, the preceding discussion and exercise will have helped participants to reflect on the reasons why this might be the case.

- Make the point that children are sometimes adopted into families ethnically and culturally different from their family of origin (perhaps because finding a "perfect match" would be impossible or would take too long). Where there are differences (great or small), adopters need to make conscious efforts to support the child's identity and other needs.

- Discuss multiple and diverse identities. Helping the child to accept and value every aspect of his identity is one of the more important tasks for adopters.

- Some children have multiple and diverse identities. For example, a child may have one parent who is Irish and one who is Asian, or one Christian parent and one Muslim parent; a child may be from an ethnic minority or an Eastern European background and also have a disability. It's important for adults involved with the child not to focus so much on one aspect of the child's identity that the other(s) is disregarded or forgotten.

- Point out that matching is complex in some situations – for example, where two siblings have been living together and need to be placed together but have fathers of different

Preparing to adopt

ethnicities. Exact ethnic matching would be impossible for both children, but an adoptive family must be able to meet the needs of both children.

- Transracial adoptions are covered in more detail in the module *The children*.

Presentation

Life story work

SLIDE What is life story work?

Life story work:

- gathers together facts about people, places and events in a child's past
- provides a structure for talking to adopted children and young people about their past
- may result in a book, film, audio tape, computer file, map with important places and dates marked on it, memory box or record of sessions
- The *process* of doing life story work is more important than the finished product

Note to trainers

As an example of a life story book, show participants a copy of *My Life and Me* by Jean Camis.

SLIDE Doing life story work

Life story work:

- can improve a child's sense of self-worth and self-esteem
- makes it clear to the child that the need for adoption was because of the actions of adults, not because he was bad or unlovable
- should tell the truth, not paint a rosy picture
- may have been done before the child came to you or may be done (or continue) afterwards with a social worker or therapist
- may need to be done (or continued) in a formal way by adopters
- will be done, informally, as part of everyday life with adopters

Linking, matching and introductions

SLIDE A new approach to life story work developed by Joy Rees

- Instead of starting with child's birth and working forwards, it starts in the present
- This reinforces child's sense of belonging with adoptive family
- Addresses child's history and early trauma
- Then brings child back to secure present and hopes for the future

Information for trainer

Joy Rees (2009) has developed a new approach to life story work that promotes a new family-friendly way to compile a life story book and one that promotes a sense of permanency for the child and encourages attachments within the adoptive family.

On her website, Joy Rees explains her model of life story work:

Instead of starting with the child's birth and early history, my model begins in the present and playfully engages the child before moving gently into the past.

My life story books aim to reinforce the child's sense of belonging and security within the adoptive family before addressing their history and early trauma. The book brings the child back to a secure present and leaves them with a sense of a positive future.

This approach stresses the child's need to be claimed and to belong, it raises the profile of adoptive parents and emphasises the importance of their involvement in contributing to the book.

SLIDE Memorabilia and their value

- Photographs and other items from the child's childhood are important
- For some children, they may be all they have to remember their birth family by
- Keep them in a way that shows that you value them
- Keep copies of documents and photos in case the child destroys them when he is feeling angry (also scan certificates and other important documents to safeguard them)

Note to trainers

For example, adopters can show they value items from the child's past by keeping them in an attractive "memory box". Photographs of the child's birth family could be put up in his bedroom or displayed in the living room alongside other family photographs if the child wishes. They could also create a special file on a computer for the child to save and access photographs, etc.

Preparing to adopt

Children's names

- Show the slide below and read out the poem.

- Discuss with the group the importance of children's names to their identity and why adopters are – in most cases – asked to retain the name the child was given by birth parents.

- Ask them what they think might be acceptable and justifiable reasons to change a child's name.

- Draw parallels between accepting the child's given name and accepting the child as he is.

SLIDE Coming home from the appointment

The one thing I did not expect was a name.
It never occurred to me that I would have been given a name.
That she loved me enough to have named me.
A beautiful name. An Irish name. A unique name.
My name.
That I was not anonymous. What will you do now?
Laugh out loud, dance through this town holding hands
with my name.

(Chanter, 2009)

Note to trainers

Naming a child is an important way of "claiming" him as your own and this issue may well arouse strong feelings within the group. The question of changing a child's name is an issue where the views of adopters sometimes diverge from those of the social work profession as a whole. Some prospective adopters may feel that, as the child's new parents, they should be "allowed" to change the child's name (especially a baby or very young child):

- if they dislike the child's name;

- if the child's name has been spelt wrongly or has a very unusual spelling;

- if they feel the name doesn't "fit" with the other family names;

- if they feel it makes the child uniquely identifiable in the present or future when the child is old enough to establish an online presence.

Sometimes social workers will share the adopters' concern that the child's birth relatives may be able to trace the child because of his unusual name. In a very small number of cases, where a baby or young child might be at risk of abduction if the birth parents were able to trace him or her, if the child's first name is unusual or is spelt in an unusual way, social

Linking, matching and introductions

workers might advise changing it. Sometimes the name could be shortened or changed only slightly. However, each case should be considered on an individual basis, based on an assessment of the actual risk, if any.

Adopters considering changing the name need to bear in mind that this will not prevent the child from searching for his birth family when he is older (see the section on social networking in the module *Telling, contact and social networking*).

When the adopters simply dislike the name, changing it is more contentious. Social workers will want to stress the importance of the name to the child's identity needs.

NB There is case law that states that children's names cannot be changed prior to an adoption order without the consent of everybody with parental rights or express direction of the court: *Re D, L and LA* (care: change of forename) Family Division (Butler-Sloss P) 24 June 2002 [2003] 1 FLR 339.

Follow-up task for after the session

- Encourage participants to reflect on their own experiences of being parented and what they would bring/leave behind if they become parents themselves. They could make notes on this in the Applicant's Workbook.

- If participants are in a couple relationship, encourage them to consider how they might differ in their parenting styles and how they might handle any differences.

To conclude

Sum up one of the key messages from today's session. It may go something like this:

Becoming a parent through adoption means your child comes to you with a name, with a birth family, possibly with a different cultural heritage, with all kinds of history that you as an adopter will need to be able to accept. He may not look like you, or like the same things the rest of your family enjoys, or be good at the same things. Can you empathise with what it is like for the child to join a new family and make this transition as easy as possible for him? Can you accept the child as he is? If you can, you will be well placed to help meet the child's identity needs and build his self-esteem. These are crucial tasks for all adoptive parents.

You may wish to end this session with a closing exercise from page 26 or an exercise of your choice.

Suggested reading for trainers

Argent H (2004) *Related by Adoption*, London: BAAF

Argent H (2006) *Ten Top Tips on Placing Children*, London: BAAF

Camis J (2001) *My Life and Me*, London: BAAF

Preparing to adopt

Cousins J (2011) *Ten Top Tips for Making Matches*, London: BAAF

Dunbar L (2009) *Ten Top Tips for Making Introductions*, London: BAAF

Fahlberg V (1994) *A Child's Journey through Placement*, London: BAAF (Chapter 4)

Gilligan R (2009) *Promoting Resilience*, London: BAAF

Maye J (2011) *Me and My Family*, London: BAAF

Rees J (2009) *Life Story Books for Adopted Children: A family-friendly approach*, London: Jessica Kingsley Publishers

Saunders H and Selwyn J with Fursland E (2013) *Placing Large Sibling Groups for Adoption*, London: BAAF

Wolfs R (2008) *Adoption Conversations: What, when and how to tell*, London: BAAF

References

Argent H (2006) *Ten Top Tips on Placing Children*, London: BAAF

Beesley P (2010) *Making Good Assessments: A practical resource guide* (second edition), London: BAAF

Chanter C (2009) 'Coming home from the appointment', in Harris P (ed) (2012) *Chosen: Living with adoption*, London: BAAF

Cousins J (2011) *Ten Top Tips for Making Matches*, London: BAAF

Department for Education (2013) *Statutory Guidance on Adoption*, London: BAAF

Dunbar L (2009) *Ten Top Tips for Making Introductions*, London: BAAF

Rees J www.thejoyoflifework.com

Romaine M, Turley T and Tuckey N (2007) *Preparing Children for Permanence: A guide to undertaking direct work for social workers, foster carers and adoptive parents*, London: BAAF

Salter A (2013) *The Adopter's Handbook*, London: BAAF

Saunders H and Selwyn J (2011) *Adopting Large Sibling Groups: The experiences of adopters and adoption agencies*, London: BAAF

Saunders H, Selwyn J with Fursland E (2013) *Placing Large Sibling Groups for* Adoption, London: BAAF

MODULE 8

Telling, contact and social networking

Timing

This module will take approximately three-and-a-half to four hours (not including refreshment breaks). If you decide to include the optional exercise – Jasmine – it will take approximately 30 minutes longer.

Setting the scene

- Introduce yourself and explain your role in the agency.
- Remind participants where this module fits into your agency's training programme.
- Refer to housekeeping (e.g. location of fire escapes and toilets, timings of breaks, finish time).
- Remind participants that they will have the opportunity to discuss all the issues in more depth with their assessing social worker and there is also likely to be further training they can attend post-approval.
- Remind participants of the ground rules (p 17) and invite them to add any other rules to the list.

What you will need

- Handouts for all the participants for the exercise *When to tell and what to tell*.
- If you are planning to include the optional exercise on page 182, you will also need copies of the handout *Jasmine* (on the CD-ROM).
- One or two copies of *Social Networking and You* (Fursland, 2013) to show to participants.

Introductions/warm-up exercise

Choose one from pp 24–26 or use a warm-up exercise of your choice.

SLIDE Learning outcomes

This module will help you to:

- Understand the lifelong nature of adoption, for everyone involved
- Appreciate the importance of birth families in the lives of adopted children
- Understand why and how you need to talk about adoption with your child

Preparing to adopt

- Consider the implications of social networking for adoptive families

Information for trainers

Social networking is a theme that you may find cropping up at various points in this module because some prospective adopters are likely to be aware of the possibility of birth relatives making contact (with them or their child) via social networking, and may be anxious about this. There is unlikely to be time in this session to cover everything they need to know about this issue, so you might like to suggest that applicants read *Facing up to Facebook: A survival guide for adoptive families* by Eileen Fursland.

Presentation

Talking about adoption with your child

- At different ages, a child will need different kinds of explanation and information about adoption.
- If the child was adopted as a baby or toddler, you need to find ways of talking about adoption as she grows so that she absorbs the information naturally over time.
- Children adopted when older will have had life story work done, which adopters can continue.
- How to share difficult and painful information with the child re: adoption, birth family; ask for help with this if you need to (from adoption support social workers, perhaps therapist).
- Later life letter.
- What happens with the letterbox system after age 18.
- Re-connecting in later life.
- In some cases, adopted teenagers re-connect with birth relatives (often starting with siblings) via social networking (more on this later).

SLIDE

Life can only be understood backwards but must be lived forwards.

Søren Kierkegaard

Telling, contact and social networking

Exercise

When to tell and what to tell

Give each participant a copy of the handout below and ask them to divide into five groups. Ask each group to consider this child at a different age: four-and-a-half, seven, 10, 13 and 17. Each group should imagine the questions Jordan might have for his adopters at this particular age and what the main issues might be for him. Each group should address the points on the handout.

After 15 minutes, ask the groups to feed back.

HANDOUT

Jordan

Jordan, aged four-and-a-half, is a bright and active child who loves watching DVDs and playing outside on his bike. His birth mother was white, of English descent, and his father was born in England to black parents who originally came from Somalia. Jordan's mother died a year ago. His father, who has serious drug and alcohol problems, is unable to care for him. Jordan has been "looked after" for one year. During this time he has been with the same foster carers.

- How might Jordan react to discussion of his birth family?
- What might he want to know at this stage and why?
- What might prevent you from giving him helpful information at this stage?

SLIDE Life cycle tasks for adopters

Adopters face different tasks at different stages of the child's life, both for themselves and for the child/young person:

- Before legal adoption
- With pre-school child
- With school-age child
- With adolescent
- When the child grows up and becomes independent

Preparing to adopt

Information for trainers

Refer participants to the diagrams in their Workbook, *Life cycle tasks for adopters*, which detail these.

Presentation

SLIDE Thinking about birth parents

- Face-to-face meetings between adopters and birth parents
- Birth parents' difficulties and circumstances
- Contested adoptions; voluntary adoptions
- Birth parents' loss and grief
- Support and counselling for birth parents
- Accepting responsibility
- Birth mothers' subsequent children
- Long-term impact on birth parents

Thinking about birth families

- Explain that in many cases there is the possibility of a face-to-face meeting between adopters and birth relatives, usually before introductions take place between the adopters and the child(ren).

- Discuss the difficulties birth parents may have had which have led to their child being removed, e.g. substance abuse/addiction, mental health issues, learning difficulties, being the victim of domestic violence, inadequate parenting skills. Many birth parents have had difficult childhoods themselves; some have been brought up in care. In many cases, meeting birth parents leaves adopters feeling that their child's birth parents are "sad" rather than "bad".

- Explain that most adoptions in the UK are contested, in that the birth parents will not have consented; in others, the birth parents agree that adoption is in the child's best interests.

- Discuss birth parents' loss and grief at losing child. For some, anger is also a strong emotion.

- Explain that support and counselling are offered to birth parents around adoption (if they choose to accept it).

- Accepting responsibility – some birth parents do, others never will.

Telling, contact and social networking

- Some birth mothers go on to have more children (who may also subsequently be adopted), always in the hope that they may be allowed to keep the next child.

- Long-term impact – guilt (for some); going through life without knowing where their child is or what he is doing; effect on their self-esteem; how do they tell people they had a child or children taken away?

Discussion

You should allow time and space here for participants to respond to the presentation. Invite participants to tell the rest of the group their thoughts and feelings about birth parents of children who need adoption.

Note to trainers

If necessary, try to encourage participants to empathise with the difficult circumstances of some birth parents' lives. Encourage them to consider why many birth parents have inadequate parenting skills and are unable to parent their children properly due to their mental health problems, substance abuse issues, etc. (rather than – as in other cases – deliberately setting out to harm, abuse or exploit the child).

Some birth parents will also go on to successfully parent subsequent children and this may then lead to confusion for the adopted child/young person. They may internalise this as rejection because they were not "good enough". This is where re-visiting life story work, later life letters and the CPR become important. Birth parents may be very different people in years to come or may have re-written the past (as we all have a tendency to do) so the young person may have conflicting accounts to resolve.

Presentation by birth family member and DVD clip

If possible, one or perhaps two birth family members who have contact with an adopted child, e.g. a parent or grandparent, could now join you to address the group. Each speaker should talk about their experience of having had their child/grandchild adopted and describe what it is like to have contact. You should agree in advance with the speakers about whether or not they are prepared to take questions from the group.

Show participants the DVD clip in which a birth mother talks about her experience of having had her child adopted.

Preparing to adopt

Presentation

The following presentation could be given either by one of the trainers or by the person in the agency who manages the letterbox contact system.

Contact

Put the following scenario to participants: if you have a partner, think about when your partner asked you to get married or move in with him/her. Imagine that he/she then went on to say, 'But you must promise you will never see your family again or have any contact with them'. How would that make you feel?

Discuss:

- the purposes of contact – it is meant to serve the interests of the *child*, not the birth parents – children's views must be taken into account;
- benefits of contact to the child for "identity" purposes;
- possible arrangements for contact: face-to-face meetings, letterbox system, mediation;
- support that is provided for contact;
- the voluntary nature of contact agreements;
- contact is not *always* desirable or achievable;
- circumstances which might mean contact is/is not appropriate;
- maintaining indirect contact can be an immensely complicated experience – for both adopters and birth relatives;
- the same difficulties that led to the child's removal (e.g. drug and alcohol problems, mental health problems) may affect people's ability to maintain successful contact after adoption;
- long-term value *to the child* of maintaining the links, if a contact agreement is set up – may be able to obtain up-to-date information about birth family at later date;
- the work of Lorne Loxterkamp (see below) on the risk of contact re-traumatising child if birth parent has not accepted responsibility for the damage they did (this is one of the reasons why letters are vetted so carefully by letterbox service);
- sibling groups and contact arrangements – different siblings may have differing needs for contact, sometimes with different birth relatives;
- contact with siblings in other adoptive families/foster families.

Telling, contact and social networking

Information for trainers

By now, participants should have taken on board the fact that some form of contact is likely to be required for the child or children they adopt. Some may feel they have no choice about this if they want to adopt. As well as emphasising children's needs and the need to comply with contact plans, you need to discuss the emotional reality for adopters and how contact is likely to impact on them and their child.

The Children and Families Act 2014 has introduced the option for the court of making a Contact or No Contact Order at the point of making the Adoption Order. It is recognised, however, that contact will usually be arranged by agreement. The court may note that an agreement has been made. Adopters or adopted children or birth relatives can ask the court at any time after the adoption order to make a Contact or No Contact Order where agreements don't work or there is unsolicited contact from birth family members. However, adopters need to also be aware that birth family members, including siblings, can also seek leave to apply for an order if adopters have not kept up with their contact agreement.

Janette Logan and Carole Smith carried out a research study on post-adoption contact in 1997–9 and as part of their research they asked adopters about the preparation they had been given. They say:

Preparation for adoption and direct contact needs to move beyond persuading prospective adopters about the benefits of contact for their children. Social workers need to anticipate issues and prepare new parents for the social and emotional challenges that they will face in "sharing" their children with birth families over time.

(Logan and Smith, 2004)

When making contact arrangements, say Logan and Smith, social workers need to include prospective adopters as *partners* in negotiating contact as early as possible.

SLIDE Contact for adopted children

- Contact can serve the needs of children who do not know or remember their birth family as well as those of older children who do

- Even children placed as babies will want to know: where did I come from? Who were my birth parents?

- Adopted children wonder: do my birth parents think about me? What are they like now?

Information for trainers

Research evidence is inconclusive on the extent to which contact is beneficial – it is impossible to generalise and opinions remain divided. The debate about contact is now a case of asking more subtle questions: what type of contact might be advisable, for whom,

Preparing to adopt

and when. Each case is different and must be carefully assessed.

The heterogeneities involved in all of this are both great and important. Thus, the contact with the biological parents may be direct and face-to-face or it may be through letters or telephone calls, and it may be supervised or unsupervised. In addition, there is heterogeneity with respect to the biological family. Contact cannot simply be reduced to whether or not there is contact with the biological mother, because the biological father, siblings and grandparents may all be involved. The pluses and minuses of contact may not be the same for each of these.

It is clear, too, that the children themselves differ in all sorts of ways, including their age at placement, their temperamental qualities, their prior experiences within the biological family, the degree to which the children are impaired in their functioning, and their views on what they want with respect to contact. Similarly, parents differ in all sorts of ways, including whether the biological parents supported or opposed adoption, whether they are currently impaired in their psychological functioning, and whether the contact might involve a risk of abuse – either physical or psychological.

These considerations must take into account the fact that the views and the wishes of all parties (the children, the adoptive families and the biological families) may well change over time and what is possible, or what seems important, at one point may look rather different at a later point. Clearly, it follows from all of these considerations that the handling of the contact needs to be carefully managed in relation to the details of the specific situation and the qualities, attitudes and feelings of the different participants. There is not, and cannot be, one standard approach that suits everyone and each situation needs careful, considered attention to what is likely to work best with this individual child and these adoptive and biological families.

(Rutter, 2004, viii–ix)

SLIDE "Contact After Adoption" study

The ongoing "Contact after Adoption" study (University of East Anglia) looked at how contact works (or doesn't work) to help parties understand each other.

When communication between adopters and birth relatives was *good*, adopters tended to identify the following benefits:

- Being able to answer child's questions, fill in gaps for child
- Gaining deeper, richer understanding of child's birth history
- Being able to show their child – now or in future – that he/she is not forgotten or rejected by birth family.

(Neil, 2004)

Telling, contact and social networking

SLIDE Letterbox contact

Adopters sometimes wonder why birth parents don't write back. Is it because they don't care? The study found:

- Some birth relatives still felt overwhelmed by emotions – 'It hurt too much to put my feelings down on paper.'
- Some just didn't know how to express what they wanted to say, or how their words would be received
- Some couldn't remember what they had been told about the letterbox system
- Some have problems with reading and writing
- Some were afraid of breaking rules, which made them appear passive
- Letterbox system and rules were seen as frustrating, restrictive, demeaning

(Neil, 2004)

SLIDE Later life letter

- The later life letter is a letter written by the social worker at the time of the adoption
- It is given to the adoptive parents to keep
- They can give it to the child when she is a teenager
- It provides a more "adult" explanation about her birth family and the reasons for and circumstances around her adoption

SLIDE The value of photographs

Information for trainers

For those (birth parents) who received them, photographs were an immense satisfaction. The direct, clear images of happy and healthy children often took on a much greater importance than anything the birth family had in writing...Some spoke of how hard it was to look at

177

Preparing to adopt

them, but the preference was very much to have them rather than not. Those who did not receive photographs often desperately wanted them...

(Neil, 2004, p 91)

Adopters have always been advised to ensure that any photographs they provide to birth relatives do not include any identifying details such as the child's school uniform (or the address of the photographic studio on the back of the print).

Now, of course, there are new considerations. In some cases, photographs provided through letterbox contact have been posted on birth parents' Facebook pages – often angering and distressing adopters. In the age of social networking and technology, which allows facial recognition and location-sharing, many adopters and social workers are questioning whether it is safe to provide photographs of an adopted child.

Adopters should understand the risk of inadvertently sharing their location via photographs. Data embedded in digital photographs (called EXIF data) give the geographical location where the photograph was taken and can, in some cases, be accessed when photographs are posted online via certain websites or sent via email.

Indeed, some agencies are no longer recommending that adopters send photographs of the child to birth relatives. Some are asking birth parents to sign an agreement to the effect that they will not post any photographs of the child (that they receive via letterbox contact) on social networking sites. This is a complex subject, beyond the scope of what can be covered here. The possible risk needs to be considered carefully on a case-by-case basis. An example of a risk assessment is provided in Eileen Fursland's book *Social Networking and Contact: How social workers can help adoptive families* (2010, pp 105–6).

You should state here whether your agency has specific policies around photographs and what those policies are.

SLIDE When is contact harmful?

- When birth parents haven't accepted the adoption and are likely to try to undermine it
- When it could lead to an unsafe person discovering the adoptive family's details and location
- When birth relatives remain a physical or sexual danger to the child
- When contact is "suffused with mendacity" (Loxterkamp, 2009), i.e. based on a lie

Information for trainers

Lorne Loxterkamp is a consultant child and adolescent psychotherapist whose concern about the orthodox view on contact with birth families led him to critically examine the arguments. He has written and spoken about the risks of contact to a child when birth

Telling, contact and social networking

parents refuse to accept responsibility for maltreating the child and maintain that they are blameless. He quotes cases of children he has seen in a clinical setting who are 'tormented by the effects of contact that is suffused with mendacity'.

Many adopted and fostered children who have suffered maltreatment at the hands of their birth parents have regular face-to-face meetings with them as well as routine communication in the form of cards or letters. It is commonly maintained that contact has to be beneficial because it is necessarily in the child's best interests in the long run, if not also immediately. But the predicament emerging from such cases of early maltreatment is that contact, the very thing that is meant to provide a remedy for harm, can itself be harmful and the likely cause of enduring emotional and psychological damage, even when it appears to be going well or well enough.

(Loxterkamp, 2009)

David Howe and Miriam Steele (2004) have also presented observational evidence on contact in which children have been traumatically abused or neglected by their birth parents. They make the following points.

- Permanently placed children who have suffered severe maltreatment may be re-traumatised when they have contact with the maltreating parent.

- Children may therefore experience the permanent carers as unable to protect them and keep them safe. This will interfere with the child's ability to develop a secure attachment with their new carers.

- Severely maltreated children who feel unsafe and insecure will continue to employ extreme psychological measures of defence, which may lead to a variety of aggressive, controlling and distancing behaviours. These behaviours place great strains on the carer–child relationship.

- Adopters who possess high levels of sensitivity, empathy and reflective attunement help children feel both safe and emotionally understood. These parenting capacities promote secure attachments and increase resilience.

- In contact cases where children suffer re-traumatisation, the need to make the child feel safe, protected and secure becomes the priority. Contact in the medium term would therefore not be indicated. This decision does not rule out the possibility of some form of contact at a later date, but this will depend on whether or not the child has achieved levels of resilience, psychological autonomy and reflective function that will equip them to deal with the emotional arousal that renewed contact with a once traumatising parent will initially trigger.

SLIDE The need to know the truth

- Adopters need to be given a clear explanation about why the children were removed from their birth parents

Preparing to adopt

- Adopted children and young people need to know the truth
- Seek adoption support if you are struggling with telling your child painful or difficult information

A failure to explain this clearly can lead to children concluding that they were mistakenly removed from a loving family. In these circumstances, continuing contact with the birth family may reinforce such beliefs and trigger difficult behaviour, which eventually undermines the adoption (Loxterkamp, 2009)

(quoted in Saunders *et al*, 2013).

SLIDE Siblings adopted into the same family

- Sharing information with siblings of different ages is complicated – information needs to be age-appropriate for each child
- Different siblings may have different contact needs
- Different siblings may have different responses to contact

SLIDE Siblings in different families

- Adopters should be told about full or half-siblings in other families
- Sooner or later, children will want to know
- When siblings are separated, plans should be made for maintaining contact
- It may be important for children to meet and get to know their siblings (if they haven't)
- Some adopters are keen to "keep the door open"
- Different siblings may have different responses to contact
- Each child's feelings and needs should be taken into account

Show DVD clips

From the DVD, show the clip that features a young adopted girl talking about contact with her siblings and its significance. Then show clip of adopted adults discussing their curiosity about their birth family and whether or not they want to trace them.

Group discussion and questions

This is an opportunity for participants to speak – ideally in an open and honest way – about their feelings about contact.

Telling, contact and social networking

Then give participants the opportunity to ask you questions about contact anonymously by providing pieces of paper for them to write down their questions and put them into a box – take out one question at a time and answer it.

Acknowledge that contact is complex and sometimes painful (for adopters and for the child) – but this doesn't *necessarily* mean it should not be happening. Address any concerns and misgivings the participants express and encourage them to discuss these issues with their assessing social worker (and with the child's social worker, when a match is made).

Janette Logan and Carole Smith (2004) stress that prospective adopters should be encouraged to express their concerns and worries so that these do not become future obstacles to facilitating contact or sources of resentment and suspicion.

Presentation

Helping children with contact

Remind participants of Schofield and Beek's "secure base model", which was covered in depth in the module, *The needs of children affected by neglect and abuse*. Ideally, most participants will have completed that module before the current module. Show the slide below and remind them that *Promoting family membership – helping children to belong* is one of the five important parenting dimensions.

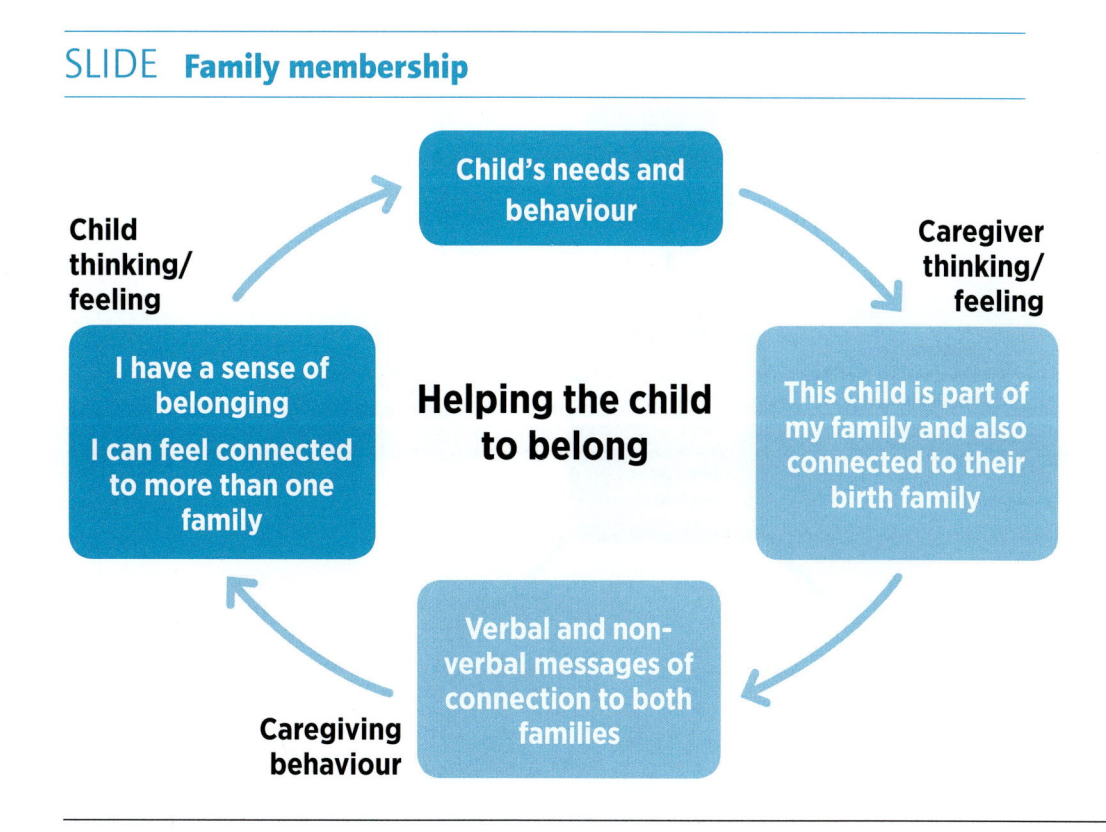

SLIDE Family membership

Helping the child to belong

- Child's needs and behaviour (Child thinking/feeling)
- Caregiver thinking/feeling: This child is part of my family and also connected to their birth family
- Caregiving behaviour: Verbal and non-verbal messages of connection to both families
- Child thinking/feeling: I have a sense of belonging; I can feel connected to more than one family

Preparing to adopt

- Remind them that in that module they considered parenting behaviour associated with promoting a feeling of family membership. They were primarily thinking about how to help a child feel that she belonged in the adoptive family.

- Say that throughout this module you are asking them to consider the child's membership of two families. Whether or not she has any form of contact with them, the chances are that she will still be thinking and wondering about her birth family, on some level, probably for the rest of her life.

- In this and other modules, we have looked at things like communicative openness, life story work and contact – these are all crucial ways in which adopters can acknowledge the child's membership of her birth family and the importance of her birth relatives.

- Refer participants to the articles in their Workbook on contact and on "telling".

Optional exercise

You may wish to include the following optional exercise if you have a number of applicants who are considering adopting older children, as these children are more likely to have direct contact with birth relatives.

Show the following slide and leave it up on the screen during the exercise.

SLIDE

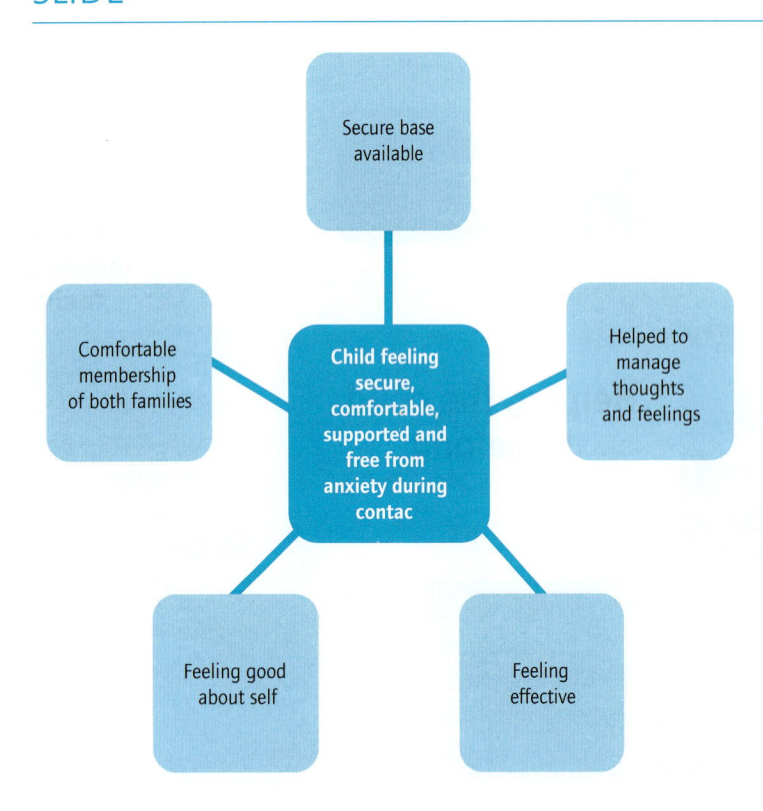

Child feeling secure, comfortable, supported and free from anxiety during contac

- Secure base available
- Helped to manage thoughts and feelings
- Feeling effective
- Feeling good about self
- Comfortable membership of both families

Telling, contact and social networking

Provide copies of the handout below and ask participants, in small groups, to discuss the scenario, think about the questions and make notes on a sheet of flip chart paper. Ask them to consider how each of the elements of sensitive caregiving can be promoted within the scenario. Suggest that they use the diagram on the slide as a prompt.

For feedback, ask each group to share what they have written. Encourage discussion and debate within the whole group – there are no "right" or "wrong" answers. It is important to think flexibly but always to bear in mind the child's perspective.

Follow up with the slide *How do sensitive caregivers help children to manage contact?*

(This exercise is featured in Beek and Schofield (2006, p 112) and the information on the slides is drawn from their work.)

HANDOUT

Jasmine

You are Jasmine's adoptive parents. Jasmine is 10 years old and is very settled in your family. Jasmine was seriously neglected in her birth family. She sees her birth parents (who have learning disabilities) every school holiday. The meetings are at a contact centre and supervised by a member of the centre staff. They seem to go smoothly but Jasmine is unsettled for at least two weeks afterwards, has nightmares and is very clingy.

- Why might Jasmine be unsettled by the contact meetings?
- What might she be thinking and feeling during and after the contact?
- What does she need now in terms of adoptive and birth family membership?
- What might help her?

SLIDE How do sensitive caregivers help children to manage contact?

- Being available – helping children to build trust
- Responding sensitively – helping children to manage feelings and behaviour
- Accepting the child – building self-esteem
- Co-operative caregiving – helping children to feel effective
- Promoting family membership – helping children to belong

Preparing to adopt

Information for trainers

How do sensitive caregivers behave in relation to contact? Explain how the parenting dimensions relate to ways in which adopters can help children to manage contact successfully.

- **Being available – helping children to build trust**
  Contact arrangements should be such that the child has access to a secure base or can hold the secure base in mind

- **Responding sensitively – helping children to manage feelings and behaviour**
  Contact is likely to involve some difficult feelings and behaviours. Adopters may need to acknowledge and contain these feelings, showing the child that they are understandable, can be coped with and made safe.

- **Accepting the child – building self-esteem**
  Contact arrangements should be such that children feel valued, accepted and good about themselves.

- **Co-operative caregiving – helping children to feel effective**
  Children need to feel appropriately included in planning and discussing contact arrangements and during contact meetings.

- **Promoting family membership – helping children to belong**
  Contact arrangements should aim to promote a comfortable sense of belonging to both families.

Presentation and quick-thinks

The internet and e-safety for children

Ask the group to imagine a time when their adopted child is old enough to start using the internet.

- All parents have the task of keeping their child safe online – ask participants to do a **quick-think** about some of the risks to children on the internet (their suggestions may include scams, bullying, online gambling, accidentally – or on purpose – accessing pornography and websites that promote violence or self-harm, as well as the risk of online grooming).

- Like all other parents, adopters will want to keep a close eye on what children are doing online and help teach them how to stay safe.

- This means taking an active interest in what they are doing and taking certain precautions (e.g. using parental controls and filters). There is plenty of advice and useful resources to be found online and elsewhere. (The Thinkuknow website (www.thinkuknow.co.uk) is a good starting point.)

- Many children set up a Facebook account when they are much younger than 13 (the age limit set by Facebook). This is easy to do. There are no checks. Parents need to be involved

Telling, contact and social networking

and supervise their children on the internet at a level appropriate to their age.

- Ask participants to do a **quick-think** and tell you all the various ways and places children and young people can access the internet: laptops, internet-enabled televisions, smartphones, games consoles, friends' laptops and smartphones, internet cafés, school and so on.

- Because of their difficulties, for example, with impulse control and managing relationships, some adopted children are particularly vulnerable to the general risks of the internet – they may be more gullible, more prone to being bullied (or bullying others), indulge in more risky behaviour and be less able to gauge whether or not other people online are genuine and can be trusted.

- Do another **quick-think**. The issue of safety on the internet may be worrying for parents, but what do they think about the idea of banning a child altogether from using the internet? Hopefully, the group will come up with views to the effect that attempting to ban a child from using the internet would be unfair, unwise and extremely difficult to enforce; it would also deprive the child of the opportunity to develop crucial IT skills; and the child who doesn't use the internet will not be able to gain the knowledge and skills to keep themselves safe online, which could lead to problems later on.

Presentation

Your child's story

- Some adopters write a blog about their experiences of adoption. These can be helpful and interesting to prospective adopters and other adopters. However, if anyone is tempted to write a blog of their own, please warn them not to post anything that could lead to their child being identified. Remind them that, if they don't heavily anonymise their blog, people will be reading about their family life – and some of the people reading it may know the adoptive family or be able to identify them from place-names and other details about the family if these are given. Remind them about protecting their personal data e.g. in online forums and blogs. The story of why the child was adopted and the difficulties it has caused her is the child's story and should not be shared carelessly.

- Families who already have birth or adopted children should also discuss these issues with them.

Preparing to adopt

Presentation

Social networking issues in adoption

SLIDE

Your presentation should cover the following.

- Adopters may have heard about cases in which birth relatives have traced adopters and adopted children/young people. They may well be apprehensive about this.

- Using Facebook, it may be possible to find someone simply by searching for their name (if the person has a Facebook account).

- Point out that most birth parents are not told the child's adoptive surname or where the family lives, so finding the child might in fact be difficult (but see pp 166–167 for advice on unusual first names).

- Internet search capabilities are becoming more powerful all the time, so a determined birth relative, who carried out a sustained search, might be able to unearth the family if he/she knows enough details about them and combines search terms. So social workers should be careful about the details they pass on to birth parents. And adopters should be careful about how much identifying information about them appears online.

- Many birth parents are still leading chaotic lives and would not have the desire or the skills to do this. Those birth parents who would want to trace their child with a view to either disrupting the adoption or "getting them back" are very few in number.

- Remind them of the need to control their privacy settings on social networking sites and consider who can see any photographs or other material they post. They may also want to ask friends and family not to post photographs of the child. If there is a risk that birth

Telling, contact and social networking

relatives might recognise them, adopters may wish to be careful about sharing photographs of themselves online too.

Quick-think

Why would adopted children and young people search online for birth relatives?

Follow this up with the following slides.

Information for trainers

Some of the group's suggestions are likely to include:

- Why *wouldn't* they? They look on the internet for everything else…
- They think it will be a quick and "easy" way to find out.
- They can do it without telling their parents (don't want to hurt them or make them angry).
- Friends may urge them or persuade them to search online.

SLIDE The need to know

- Adopted children's curiosity can surge in puberty
- Story they were told when younger no longer meets their needs
- They want *up-to-date* information

SLIDE Unanswered questions

- What are my birth family doing now?
- Where are they?
- What kind of people are they?
- Do they think about me at all?
- Do I have siblings – how are they?

In the absence of contact, adopters may not be able to answer questions.

Preparing to adopt

SLIDE The teenage years

- Adolescence is often a period of turbulent feelings, volatile behaviour, asserting independence, wanting to do things your own way, working out "who am I?"
- All of this can lead to conflict with parents.
- There are additional issues that make the teenage years even more of a rollercoaster in adoptive families.

Information for trainers

- Secrecy and silence in the adoptive family – about the child's birth family, about the circumstances of the adoption – could drive a child to want to find out more at some stage, often at puberty.
- Even if information has been fully shared, if nothing has been heard from the birth family for years the adopted young person is likely to wonder about them and want *current* information.
- Adolescence is a time when many young people start to think more deeply about their identity – they need to work out who they are and why they are the kind of people they are. It is not surprising that adopted teenagers often start feeling much more curious about their birth family at this time.
- Adopters need to ensure that they give age-appropriate information about why the child needed to be adopted. Otherwise the young person is left wanting and needing more information than the simple version which sufficed when she was a child. She will start to realise that there is "more to it than that". If her adopters cannot or do not provide answers to her questions (questions which she may not even express openly), she may decide to look on the internet and see if she can find any information about her birth relatives.

SLIDE Long-term value of contact

- It means you can find answers to your child's questions
- It keeps the door open for further contact in the future if your child wants it
- The child/young person may feel no need to search online for birth parents – she already knows how to contact them

SLIDE Communicative openness

- Contact is not always possible.
- "Communicative openness" is crucial.

Telling, contact and social networking

Information for trainers

Maintaining and re-opening contact, and social networking issues

- In many cases, contact arrangements are made, but for one reason or another, contact does not continue. If contact has been set up, maintaining this over the long term means that there is an open line of communication with the birth relatives if the child has questions later on.

- Sometimes contact is not desirable or possible. But adopters can still try to be as open as possible. Adopters can reassure their child by letting her know that they will do their best to get answers for her (via an intermediary at the agency) if she ever wants up-to-date information about her birth family. In some cases, providing this information is enough for her and she is content to leave meeting up until much later.

- David Brodzinsky, professor of psychology and eminent expert on adoption in the United States, wrote that it is the attitude and behaviour of adopters with regards to talking and thinking about adoption – their "communicative openness" – that is the key consideration. In other words, even if it's not possible to have contact with birth family members, adopters can show their child that they empathise with her experience of being adopted; are comfortable about adoption; recognise the importance of her birth family members to her; and are happy to talk about it and answer her questions (or find answers for her).

- Maintaining contact also means that it may be possible to arrange for the child to re-connect with her birth relatives when she is older, perhaps when she is a teenager and feels the need to find out more or perhaps is even keen to meet them. Not all children and young people will want this. Stress that with children under 18 adopters should, of course, ask for help and support with this from the adoption agency.

SLIDE Who contacts whom?

- Many cases of Facebook contact between adopted young people and birth relatives are initiated *by young people themselves*. In a few cases, this has happened with children as young as 11 or 12.

- What does this mean for adopters?

SLIDE Social networking: some other points

- Sometimes siblings who have been separated find each other
- Adopted children and young people need to be informed about what might happen
- Contact, when it happens this way, can be overwhelming and disrupting

Preparing to adopt

- Adopters need to have "what if...?" conversations with older children
- If necessary, a No Contact Order can be made

Information for trainers

The idea that some adopted children will want to find and make contact with their birth families in the teenage years is likely to be a difficult one for prospective adopters to take on board. Many will be alarmed at the idea that a birth relative could come into their child's life via social networking, while the child is still so young, and with no intermediary. You will need to tread carefully to address their understandable fears and anxieties.

You need to let them know what they can do to try to reduce the risks, while acknowledging that there are some things that it is not always possible to control.

It's important that prospective adopters take on board the implications of the fact that many cases of unmediated contact are initiated by young people themselves. For example, changing the child's name when she is first adopted will not prevent later social networking contact with birth family members *that is initiated by the adopted young person.*

Why children need to know the truth

It's important for children to know what happened to them at the hands of their birth family. They need to hear the truth, in an age-appropriate way – not least because there is a chance that some of them may re-connect with birth relatives at some point, perhaps doing this online and in secret in their teenage years.

If adopted young people have not been told the full story (perhaps adopters have found it too difficult to tell or have wanted to protect them from painful truths), there is a risk that they will make contact with birth relatives without the knowledge that certain individuals abused them in their early childhood.

Some birth relatives may "rewrite history" and present a sanitised or untrue version of events, which can be deeply disturbing and confusing for the adopted young person.

If there is a possibility of an older child or teenager making contact in an unplanned way with parents who abused them, adopters should of course seek help from the adoption agency.

Have "what if...?" conversations

Adopters need to explicitly discuss with older children the implications of social networking contact with birth relatives. They need to have "what if...?" conversations: for example, 'What would you do if your birth sister found you on Facebook?'; 'What would you do if you got a message from your birth mother?' This may help the child to think through the possible consequences and alternatives. Adoptive parents need to have conversations with their adopted teenagers about the risks and pitfalls of making direct contact via social networking sites rather than by using intermediary services.

Telling, contact and social networking

At this point, you may wish to show participants a copy of *Social Networking and You* (Fursland, 2013), a booklet written for adopted young people, which can be used to open up such conversations.

To conclude

What do adopters say?

In a Twitter chat on adoption, adopters were asked to sum up in three words what adoption meant for them. Some of their responses are on the slide below. You may wish to end the session by asking applicants to sum up, in three words, how they themselves are feeling about what lies ahead.

SLIDE What adoption means for me

Adopters were asked to sum up, in three words, what adoption means for them:

My lovely family

Simply our boys

Truly life-changing

Our family complete

Best thing ever

Never look back

SLIDE One adopter's message to those considering adoption:

Don't be scared by the negatives – it truly is the best thing we've ever done.

Suggested reading for trainers

Fursland E (2013) *Facing up to Facebook: A survival guide for adoptive families* (second edition), London: BAAF

Fursland E (2010) *Social Networking and Contact: How social workers can help adoptive families*, London: BAAF

Fursland E (2013) *Social Networking and You* (second edition), London: BAAF

Wolfs R (2008) *Adoption Conversations: How, when and what to tell*, London: BAAF

References

Beek M and Schofield G (2006) *Attachment for Foster Care and Adoption: A training programme*, London: BAAF

Fursland E (2010) *Social Networking and Contact: How social workers can help adoptive families*, London: BAAF

Howe D and Steele M (2004) 'Contact in cases in which children have been traumatically abused or neglected by their birth parents', in Neil E and Howe D (eds) *Contact in Adoption and Permanent Foster Care: Research, theory and practice*, London: BAAF

Logan J and Smith C (2004) 'Direct post-adoption contact: experiences of birth and adoptive families', In Neil E and Howe D (eds) *Contact in Adoption and Permanent Foster Care: Research, theory and practice*, London: BAAF

Loxterkamp L (2009) 'Contact and truth: the unfolding predicament in adoption and fostering', *Clinical Child Psychology & Psychiatry*, 14, pp 423–435

Neil E (2004) 'The "Contact after Adoption" study: indirect contact and adoptive parents' communication about adoption', in Neil E and Howe D (eds) *Contact in Adoption and Permanent Foster Care: Research, theory and practice*, London: BAAF

Rutter M (2004) 'Foreword', in Neil E and Howe D (eds) *Contact in Adoption and Permanent Foster Care: Research, theory and practice*, London: BAAF

Saunders H and Selwyn J with Fursland E (2013) *Placing Large Sibling Groups for Adoption: A good practice guide*, London: BAAF

MODULE 9

Life as an adoptive family: learning to live together

Timing

This module will take between three and three-and-a-half hours, not including refreshment breaks.

Setting the scene

- Introduce yourself and explain your role in the agency.
- Remind participants where this module fits into your agency's training programme.
- Refer to housekeeping (e.g. location of fire escapes and toilets, timings of breaks, finish time).
- This module aims to help participants consider life with their adopted child, from the early days right through to adolescence and beyond.
- Remind participants that they will have the opportunity to discuss all the issues in more depth with their assessing social worker and there is also likely to be further training they can attend post-approval.
- Remind participants of the ground rules (page 17) and invite them to add any other rules to the list.

What you will need

- For this module, you will need to provide handouts for all the participants for the exercise *The origins of challenging behaviour in children*, and some copies of the Adoption Passport.
- You may also like to have a copy of *Understanding Why: Understanding attachment and how this can affect education with special reference to adopted children and young people and those looked after by local authorities* (published by National Children's Bureau and available from the website www.ncb.org.uk) to show to the group.
- If this is the final session of the course, have evaluation forms for the participants to complete at the end. You will find an example on the CD-ROM or your agency may use its own evaluation form.

Preparing to adopt

SLIDE Learning outcomes

This module will help you to:

- Think about what early days with your adopted child might bring
- Consider behavioural strategies children may have developed to survive past abuse and/or neglect
- Know more about your likely need for support and how you can access this
- Consider the needs of an adopted child in school

Exercise

What you are looking forward to

As a positive warm-up exercise at this point, you could ask participants in small groups to think about – and share with members of their group – the things they are most looking forward to about adopting a child.

Quick-think: The early days – post-placement blues

Living with a child or children is a major life change and some adopters experience "post-placement blues" in the early days. Make it clear that this is normal. Equally, they may experience a honeymoon period!

Unlike in postnatal depression, there is no hormonal component to post-placement blues – but some of the other factors may be common to new parents who have had a baby. Ask the group for some suggestions about possible reasons for some adopters feeling less than joyful a few weeks into the adoption.

Note to trainers

Some of the suggestions may include, for example:

- loss of freedom;
- no spare time;
- lack of sleep;
- overwhelming sense of responsibility;
- caring for the child can be exhausting and thankless;
- sense of anti-climax after hoping for and working towards this for so long;

Life as an adoptive family

- loss of previous role in job/career;
- realising you are not the "super-parent" you hoped you might be;
- "starting at Chapter 2" – coming to terms with the fact that you have not given birth and (in some cases) have missed out on this child's babyhood;
- empathising with the birth parents' loss;
- major life change – "what have we done?"

Remind the group that the aim of this course and of the assessment is to ensure they have realistic expectations, but in a sense it's impossible to fully prepare a person for what it will feel like to become a parent. There are some things that can only be learned by experience. Reassure them that most new and adoptive parents adjust in time to their new life. Meanwhile, they shouldn't be afraid of asking for help if things are tough.

Presentation

What if you don't feel love for the child?

Your presentation should cover the following points:

- Not everyone instantly falls in love with the child they are adopting. For some, it takes time.
- The everyday caring tasks you do for your child will help build the bonds between you over the weeks, months and years. Sometimes you need to just get on with doing the physical caring and nurturing and, in time, love grows.
- It may take longer than you expect for the child to reciprocate your affection and love.

You may want to refer to the example below.

Note to trainers

By this stage, participants may have learned about attachment and attachment disorders and will be starting to accept that some children will not be able to form new bonds quickly or easily. However, the thought that they themselves might struggle to love the child could be worrying for them.

If you happen to have an adopter as one of the trainers, who has experienced this and who is happy to present this section and discuss their own feelings, it can be very powerful for participants to hear this from the adopter.

Alternatively, you could read out to them the example below, which will encourage applicants to realise that these feelings are not abnormal and need not spell the end of the placement. You can also remind them that they can talk over their feelings with their social worker.

Preparing to adopt

One adopter of a sibling group described how her social worker had saved the placement by saying 'a really helpful thing'.

'I remember saying to her one day… – and I was really worried about saying it – '" don't think I love (child). I don't love her because there is nothing there – I don't feel anything is happening." And I fully expected them to say, "Right, that's it. Let's end it." But of course instead she said, "Well, you may never love her, and she may never love you, but what you've got is you've given her sibling relationships." And because she said that, that took the pressure off me and I was able subsequently to form a relationship – but if she had been… blaming and cold towards me about that, I'm not sure that the placement…would have lasted. In fact, I'm sure it wouldn't have done…I suddenly didn't have to feel like the worst mother in the universe because I couldn't love this poor little girl who had been through all these dreadful things…I thought, 'Oh yeah, actually she's getting quite a lot out of being here'.

(Saunders and Selwyn with Fursland, 2013)

Exercise

The origins of challenging behaviour in children

Give participants the handouts (below) of case studies about children's behaviour. These case studies feature abnormal, aggressive or otherwise disturbed behaviour in children. Ask participants to discuss the following questions:

- How do you feel about this behaviour?
- Why do you think it might be happening?
- What would you do in this case?

A spokesperson from each group should feed back on the range of feelings and ideas from his or her group.

Point out that becoming an adopter does not make you superhuman – you will still sometimes feel angry or upset by certain behaviour. But having an understanding of why the child might be behaving in that way could help you cope with your feelings and prevent you from blaming yourself or feeling that you have somehow failed.

Remind participants that some children may need professional therapeutic help at some point in their childhood – possibly soon after the adoption or perhaps some years later.

Life as an adoptive family

HANDOUTS

Zoe

Zoe is only four but insists on doing everything for herself. She will not let you help her dress or tie her shoes and when you insist, she tries to push you away and gets upset. If she hurts herself, she will not accept comfort and she rarely cries. Bath times are a major hassle and frequently end up with tears or sulks. Her favourite phrase seems to be 'I'll do it'.

Heather

Heather is nearly seven. You know that she was sexually abused by her stepfather.

When Heather first came to live with you nearly six months ago, she used to try to sit on your knee all the time and, if your wife was out of the room, would try to kiss you on the mouth. She has learned to ask for cuddles more appropriately now and will sit quietly beside you on a sofa leaning against you to listen to a story or watch television.

Today you have a joiner working in your house. Heather has been watching him work, has chatted brightly with him and has now gone into the garden to play. While she is outside, he comes to tell you that she has just said he has a 'lovely bum' and has tried to touch him.

Carl

Carl (seven) was removed from his parents' care and lived with foster carers before he came to live with you 18 months ago. Since then, you have been worried that he suggests that anyone who upsets him, including his teacher, should 'have their head cut off' or 'get cut in two'. You have tried to tell him that that is not the way to sort things out, but he remains very interested in violence such as car crashes, murder or riots featured on television.

Your three-year-old nephew comes to visit for the weekend and you find Carl has put him in the wendy house in the garden and is poking him with a sharp stick thrust through the window. The child is distressed but Carl is laughing and obviously excited.

Javid

You have recently adopted Javid, who is five years old. He eats everything you put in front of him but he also takes food from the fridge and cupboards without asking you and stashes it away in his room under the bed. You discovered a pile of mouldy food there and asked him not to do it again, but he is still doing it. You have recently been told by the school that Javid is taking food from the other children's lunchboxes at school. When you ask him about this, he denies it.

Preparing to adopt

Anthony

Five-year-old Anthony has been with you for six months. He wants to be with you the whole time and is clingy and whiney when he wants something. Your mother-in-law is staying with you and suggests that what Anthony needs is a good smack. You have been told that at school he has difficulty getting on with the other children because he always wants to dominate the game and control what the other children do.

Nadia

Nadia is a nine-year-old girl. She has been with you since the age of nine months. She was rejected by her birth parents; she was born as the result of an affair her mother had with a much older man. Nadia has two older siblings who remained with her parents. Nadia is developing well physically and intellectually. She is very volatile emotionally, has frequent temper tantrums and can be aggressive towards other children and adults. She shows no remorse when she hurts others. She even seems pleased when she hurts you. She is physically aggressive and excitable in groups, and unable to follow social norms such as taking turns. If thwarted, Nadia screams. You have been asked to go to a meeting at school where you are told that the school is no longer able to contain Nadia's behaviour and is excluding her for three days. They are talking about a permanent exclusion if this behaviour continues.

Charmaine

Six-year-old Charmaine has recently been placed with you, along with her younger siblings, twin boys aged two. She is determined to do everything for her brothers and is constantly telling you that 'they won't eat that, they don't like it' or 'you're doing it wrong, you have to do it this way.' She doesn't seem interested in playing and often gets angry with you. She won't stop telling you what to do and how to do it – every day feels like a power struggle.

SLIDE Possible reasons for difficult behaviour in adopted children

- Disturbed by transition from foster care
- Fear of abandonment or of being moved again
- Grieving for loss of birth parents/foster carers and others
- Impact of abuse and neglect on child's brain development
- Specific conditions, e.g. attention deficit hyperactivity disorder
- Behaviour patterns child has developed in past, which are not appropriate now
- Oldest child of sibling group has been "parenting" younger siblings

Life as an adoptive family

Information for trainers

Some difficult behaviour or regression to earlier ways of behaving may be linked to the stress of moving to an adoptive family and settling in. Adopters may well be able to cope with this fairly easily, with advice and support from adoption social workers and others (e.g. experienced adopters).

But remind participants that other difficult behaviour may be linked to the impact of emotional, physical or sexual abuse or neglect on the child's social, cognitive and emotional development, leading to long-term difficulties with impulse control, anger or lack of empathy; it may be linked to fear of abandonment or anger at having been rejected or mistreated.

Some problematic behaviour is rooted in strategies that the child has adopted as a survival mechanism in his or her birth family. For example, it's easy to see why a child might need to hoard food if he or she has been in a family where food was sometimes withheld as a punishment or if the child could never be sure if there would be food on the table. A child may have learned to lie to stay out of trouble. Some aspects of behaviour (e.g. clinginess and whining or over-controlling behaviour) may have developed as a result of a helpless child's attempts to find a way of getting a neglectful adult to attend to their needs. These behaviours can persist for some time, even when the child is in a loving family.

Some children have always had to take care of younger siblings, in the absence of a competent parent. One adopter with a "parentified" child who was reluctant to relinquish responsibility for her siblings found the strategy that worked was to say to the child:

'Right, you show me how you do it and I'll follow you'. And that way she backed off, because she thought I was doing it the right way, and ...after a matter of probably three or four weeks she gave up anyway. She was too busy playing and enjoying herself.

(Saunders *et al*, 2013, p 71)

Presentation

Positive interventions

Your presentation should cover the following points:

Behaviour that seems similar may stem from different origins, so effective intervention depends on discovering the origin.

But all effective intervention aims to:

- promote attachment
- reinforce positive behaviour
- physically stop dangerous behaviour

Preparing to adopt

- avoid risky situations for both the child and the adult

And there are some basic principles:

- Don't accuse or demand reasons for negative behaviour. Offer to help the child work out why he or she behaved like that.
- Offer help to the child in controlling his or her behaviour.
- Provide a "nurturing" living experience which meets underlying needs. Basic needs must be met *unconditionally* – not because the child has been good, but because meeting needs is good for children.
- Behaviour modification does not work with children with a poor sense of "self-worth" – they do not believe they deserve rewards.
- Adults need to initiate positive interaction.
- Behaviour modification is more useful for "habit" behaviour. It is easier to reinforce good behaviour than decrease bad behaviour.

SLIDE Managing behaviour problems

NO

- to control battles
- to ridicule
- to ignoring the child
- to rejection, however brief

Information for trainers

Specific approaches are needed for different behaviour problems. There is a need to differentiate between discipline and punishment.

NB Interventions that might be useful with children who have a healthy attachment will not necessarily have the same effect on a child who has been neglected or abused and who has attachment problems. For example, telling a child with a healthy attachment to "go to your room" might effectively change behaviour, because the child will react to the disapproval from the adult attachment figure and will not enjoy enforced separation from people who are important to him or her. A child who has not developed an attachment will not have the same reaction to disapproval and may actually be relieved to be away from adults who make emotional demands.

Life as an adoptive family

Participants will also learn (or will have learned) about building resilience and using various therapies for children in the module, *The needs of children affected by neglect and abuse.*

Presentations from invited speakers

Support for adoptive families

1. The Adoption Support Services Adviser (ASSA)

The ASSA or someone from the agency's adoption support team should address the group, covering the following:

- Explanation of Adoption Passport
- Outline of support the agency can provide
- How to identify your support needs
- Knowing what you are entitled to
- How to ask for the support you need at any stage before, during or after placement
- How to access other support in the community, and who can help you with this
- Accessing therapy
- Education (where to find information and support, getting a school place, extra classroom support, pastoral care)
- Being an advocate for your child

2. Speaker from Adoption UK

A representative of Adoption UK could be invited to address the group and explain what support the organisation offers to adoptive parents, e.g. online forum, local groups, training courses and so on.

3. Presentation from an adopter

An experienced adopter whom you have invited should talk to the group about his or her own experience of getting support/therapy for an adopted son or daughter with emotional/behavioural difficulties.

You can also refer participants to their Workbook in which there are articles about the experiences of adopters.

Preparing to adopt

Adopted children in school

Quick-think

Ask the group for their thoughts and ideas about what things might be particularly difficult about school for an adopted child. Draw on these and add any further points in your presentation (below).

Presentation

Adopted children in school

It may be helpful here to show applicants the leaflet *Understanding Why: Understanding attachment and how this can affect education with special reference to adopted children and young people and those looked after by local authorities* (National Children's Bureau). Tell them that it is available online from www.ncb.org.uk if they would like their own copy.

SLIDE Adopted children and education

- The child's history will have an impact on his intellectual development
- Premature birth; medical complications; disability
- Early home environment – parents may not have talked to or read to the child – poor language and communication skills
- Long absences from school (for some older adopted children)
- Emotional and behavioural problems impact on ability to sit still, listen, concentrate

SLIDE The school environment

- Choose the right school for your child. What kind of school would he like?
- Adopted children have priority for school admissions
- Get to know child's teacher and ensure they are aware of subjects child might find difficult or upsetting (e.g. family trees, genetics)
- Help teacher understand how to help child cope with challenging situations
- Losses and transitions – between classes or schools – can be particularly difficult
- "Trauma triggers" in school and issues related to attachment

Life as an adoptive family

- Managing peer group relationships
- What will child tell classmates about his history, his adoption?

SLIDE Many adopted children need extra support with learning

You may need to be an advocate for your child to get the school or other agencies to provide the support he needs.

Adopted children qualify for the Pupil Premium – financial assistance for the school to meet the child or young person's educational needs.

SLIDE Safety in school

- If, in your child's case, there is a risk that he might be identified in the local community, inform school he must not feature in school photographs, videos or local media
- Consider the possibility of child's school friends posting photos of him on social networking sites; what precautions are needed, if any?

Information for trainers

The slides and information in this section on adopted children in school are adapted from *Ten Top Tips for Supporting Education* (Fursland *et al*, 2013).

- When the child moves in with adopters it is best if he can start in his new school at the beginning rather than in the middle of term.
- Adopters should be aware that lessons on certain subjects could be upsetting for the child, for example, being asked to bring in a photograph of himself as a baby (he may not have any); to write an autobiography; to write an essay entitled "My family"; or to design a family tree.
- Lessons on genetics, sex education and drugs education may remind a child or young person (e.g. one who has been sexually abused or whose birth parents misused drugs) of behaviour of birth relatives. A child who has suffered sexual abuse may be much more knowledgeable than his/her peers and make inappropriate comments in lessons, or may be upset by the lesson's content.
- For a child who has suffered many losses in his life, a favourite teacher or close friend leaving the school can be particularly hard and may rekindle memories of past losses.
- The child may be unsure of how or how much to tell his schoolmates about his past or his adoption. He may share too much and then find that they fail to respect confidences or use the information to bully him.

Preparing to adopt

- Certain things in school might trigger traumatic memories. For instance, for a child who has been sexually abused, showering after PE might be frightening.

- Refer to the section in Module 8 on social networking. For older children, social networking might compromise confidentiality of placement.

Training for new teachers does not devote much time to attachment disorder or the effects on children of trauma, grief and loss. So teachers may not have a good understanding of why some children behave the way they do. They may simply see a defiant and disruptive young person, not the damaged and hurt child inside.

If a child is having behavioural issues in school and possibly getting into trouble, adopters will need to work with school staff to help them understand where the child's difficulties come from and what strategies might work with him. Adopters may need to be an advocate for their child in the education system.

When living or working with a traumatised child, the issue is not "what to do" but rather "how to be". A calm teacher who expresses his or her own feelings appropriately and stays in control of the emotional tone of the environment can create a feeling of safety and security, which will help to soothe the child's hyperarousal, fear or anger.

Of course, there may be times when a child or young person has to leave the classroom because their behaviour is unacceptably disruptive or because they are putting themselves or others at risk. The school will have a protocol for dealing with incidents like this, which will involve removing the child from the classroom and sending him to someone else, so that the teacher can continue to teach the rest of the class. In the case of a traumatised child, this protocol should ideally acknowledge and address the child's difficulties and should aim to help him to learn from the incident.

(Fursland *et al*, 2013, pp 69–70)

Some schools commission school-based mental health support for pupils with emotional and behavioural problems. This can be done in partnership with a range of different agencies. There may be one-to-one support, lunchtime drop-in services for children and training and advice for teachers.

The voice of the child: discussion with adopted teenagers

This should take the form of a panel discussion with three young adopted people forming the "panel". It should be chaired either by one of the trainers or by someone who knows the young people well, e.g. an adoption support worker.

The teenagers should ask questions and raise issues that the participants will need to consider if they go on to adopt. Then the participants themselves have the opportunity to ask questions of the adopted teenagers.

At the end of the discussion, thank the teenagers for their help. Celebrate the fact that they have flourished and blossomed into such delightful young people!

Life as an adoptive family

Note for trainers

This section of the module has been included at the end of the day to allow the teenagers time to get to the venue after school or college.

This is an opportunity for prospective adopters to meet adopted teenagers and consider issues they may not have thought of before. It's also a reminder that adoption is a lifelong experience and the baby, toddler or young child they adopt will one day be a teenager with very definite views of their own!

It would be a good idea to agree in advance with the teenagers the questions they would like to ask, to avoid any surprises. The teenagers should be debriefed afterwards by the person who chairs the panel.

Make it clear to the teenagers in advance that they do not have to answer specific questions from the participants if they would rather not share certain information or if this would make them feel uncomfortable.

To conclude

Finish the session by encouraging participants to look to the future with hope. For some or perhaps most of the adopters in the group, this will be their final session, so congratulate them on everything they have learned and achieved and thank them for all that they have contributed during the course. Send them off with your good wishes. Your message could be along the following lines:

Adoption is the start of a new life together. From the point of placement, your life will revolve around your child or children – as indeed it does for most parents when they become a family. You will come up against situations you could never have predicted. Sometimes you will wonder what you have taken on. But you won't be alone – there are people to help and support you. Children bring joy, fun, fulfilment, pride and, yes, sometimes headaches and heartache, for the rest of your life. By your love, commitment and nurturing, you can make a real difference to the children you adopt, for the rest of their lives. We wish you all well for the future.

If this is the final session of the preparation course, ask participants to complete the evaluation form available on the CD-ROM for you to print off.

Show DVD clips

Show clips of three sets of adopters on how adoption has changed their lives.

Preparing to adopt

End this session by reading out the following quote and poem.

SLIDE Parenting by adoption

Relationships with parents last a lifetime. They remain of fundamental importance to children whose lives have been transformed by the opportunity to love and be loved. The adopter's story is ultimately an uplifting tale of love which is unconditional, care which is warm and commitment which is lifelong.

(Howe, 1996, p 141)

SLIDE

*Not flesh of my flesh, nor bone of my bone,
But still miraculous… my own
Never forget for a single minute, you grew not under my heart, but in it.*

(Unknown author)

Suggested reading for trainers

National Children's Bureau (undated) *Understanding Why: Understanding attachment and how this can affect education with special reference to adopted children and young people and those looked after by local authorities,* London: NCB

Neil E and Howe D (2004) *Contact in Adoption and Permanent Foster Care: Research, theory and practice,* London: BAAF

References

Fursland E with Cairns K and Stanway C (2013) *Ten Top Tips for Supporting Education,* London: BAAF

Howe D (1996) *Adopters on Adoption,* London: BAAF

Saunders H and Selwyn J with Fursland E (2013) *Placing Large Sibling Groups for Adoption,* London: BAAF